MACMILLAN
PRE-INTER

RUTH RENDELL

Shake Hands For Ever

Retold by John Escott

MACMILLAN READERS

PRE-INTERMEDIATE LEVEL

Founding Editor: John Milne

The Macmillan Readers provide a choice of enjoyable reading materials for learners of English. The series is published at six levels – Starter, Beginner, Elementary, Pre-intermediate, Intermediate and Upper.

Level Control
Information, structure and vocabulary are controlled to suit the students' ability at each level.

The number of words at each level:

Starter	about 300 basic words
Beginner	about 600 basic words
Elementary	about 1100 basic words
Pre-intermediate	about 1400 basic words
Intermediate	about 1600 basic words
Upper	about 2200 basic words

Vocabulary
Some difficult words and phrases in this book are important for understanding the story. Some of these words are explained in the story, some are shown in the pictures, and others are marked with a number like this: ...[3]. Words with a number are explained in the *Glossary* at the end of the book.

Answer Keys
Answer Keys for the *Points for Understanding* and *Exercises* sections can be found at www.macmillanenglish.com/readers.

Contents

	A Note About The Author	4
	A Note About The Story	5
	The People In This Story	7
1	Murder!	9
2	An Angry Man	15
3	Nancy Lake	19
4	Questions about Fingerprints	24
5	Mark Somerset	29
6	A Shock for Hathall	33
7	A Very Small Fraud	37
8	Eileen Hathall	41
9	Wexford Gets Help	47
10	The Necklace	53
11	The Girl	57
12	The Wages Fraud	61
13	The Missing Woman	65
14	The Bank Accounts	70
15	The Day Before Christmas Eve	73
16	The Woman in the Pub	76
17	The Last Surprise	80
	Points for Understanding	83
	Glossary	87
	Exercises	91

A Note About The Author

Ruth Rendell is often called the 'Queen of Crime[1]'. Her books and short stories have been translated into twenty-five languages. Some have been filmed. Many of the Inspector Wexford stories have been televised and shown in countries across the world. They starred the British actor George Baker as Detective Inspector[2] Reginald Wexford.

Ruth Rendell was born on the 17th February, 1930 in South Woodford, London. Her parents were teachers. She began her writing career as a journalist, working for newspapers in Essex. Her first book, *From Doon With Death*, was published in 1964. It introduced Detective Inspector Reginald Wexford, and he soon became one of crime fiction's[3] most famous detectives. *Shake Hands For Ever* is one of twenty-two Inspector Wexford novels.

Ruth Rendell has also written a number of novels under the pen-name of 'Barbara Vine'. Barbara is Ruth Rendell's middle name. Vine was the name of her great-grandmother.

The Barbara Vine stories are generally longer and more detailed than the Ruth Rendell stories. They don't always have a murder[4] in them, and they are often set partly in the past.

Ruth Rendell has won several awards and prizes for her work, including the Crime Writers' Association Diamond, Gold and Silver 'Daggers', and the *Sunday Times* Literary Award. She has also won the Mystery Writers of America Edgar Allen Poe Award.

Ruth Rendell lives in London and writes every morning for four hours. She produces two novels a year.

A Note About The Story

Chief Inspector Reginald Wexford lives and works in the mid-Sussex town of Kingsmarkham, in south-eastern England. Kingsmarkham is a fictional town – it is not real. When some of the stories were televised, the town of Romsey in Hampshire was chosen because it was very much like the 'Kingsmarkham' of the Ruth Rendell stories. It is a very 'English' market town, with a beautiful church and plenty of wonderful countryside nearby. And Wexford is very much like an English country-town policeman. He is more interested in people and the reasons for their crimes, than in forensic evidence[5] or 'clues'.

In *Shake Hands For Ever* Wexford has to spend some time in London. But he is not really comfortable in large cities, and he quite often gets lost. Many areas of London are mentioned in the novel. These include Balham (south London), Hampstead and Kilburn (north London), Chelsea and Piccadilly (central London), Notting Hill and Earl's Court (west London).

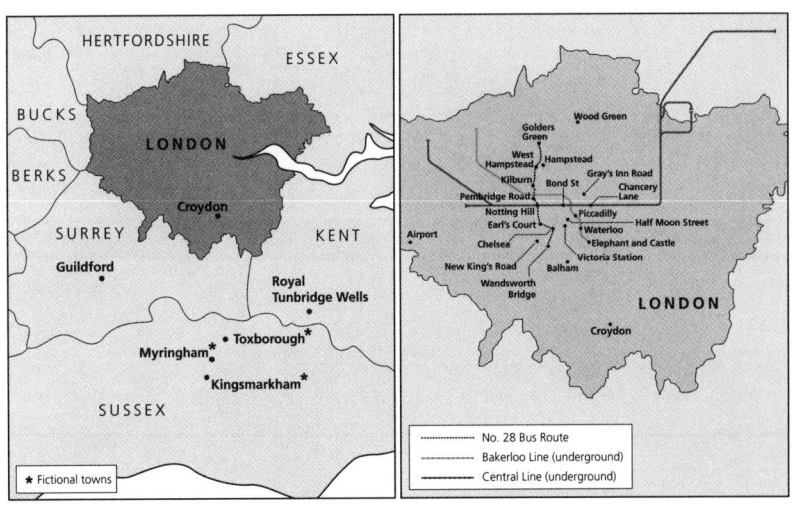

A Note About The Story

Wexford is married to Dora. Their marriage is a happy one, but Wexford is not an easy man to live with. He can be stubborn[6]. Wexford and Dora have two grown-up daughters, Sylvia and Shelia.

The title of *Shake Hands For Ever* is taken from part of a poem by the English Poet, Michael Drayton (1563–1631). The line reads:

Shake hands for ever, cancel all our vows[1],
And when we meet at any time again
Be it not seen in either of our brows[2]
That we one jot[3] *of former love retain*[4].

1 promises
2 forehead / faces
3 bit
4 keep

The People In This Story

Reg Wexford

Burden

Howard Fortune

Charles Griswold

Lovat

Hutton and Martin

Ginge Matthews

Dora Wexford

Robert Hathall

Angela Hathall

Mrs Hathall
(*Robert Hathall's mother*)

Rosemary Hathall

Eileen Hathall

Morag Grey

Nancy Lake

Mark Somerset

1
Murder!

The woman at Victoria station was waiting for her son. Robert Hathall was one minute late, but this quietly pleased the woman. Other people's faults[7] often pleased her.

'There you are,' she said, when he arrived.

'Have you got your ticket?' asked Robert.

She hadn't. She knew that he'd had money problems for the three years of his second marriage, but that was *his* fault.

'Go and buy them, or we'll miss the train,' she said.

Perhaps they *would* miss the train to Kingsmarkham. Then Angela, Robert's wife, would be angry with him. It would be a good start to the weekend, she thought with a smile.

They did not miss the train. But it was crowded, and they had to stand.

'Angela is looking forward to seeing you,' said Robert.

Mrs Hathall remembered the only time that she had met her daughter-in-law[8]. It was in a flat at Earl's Court. Angela had described Robert's first wife, Eileen, as a greedy[9] cow. Mrs Hathall had immediately walked out of the building. She told herself that she never wanted to see Angela again.

But here she was, going to Kingsmarkham. And Robert was getting nervous. 'Angela's been cleaning the house to make it nice for you,' he said.

Mrs Hathall wanted to say, 'A good wife *always* has a clean house, not just when a visitor is coming.' But she said nothing.

'Angela's meeting us with the car,' Robert said, when they arrived at Kingsmarkham railway station.

His mother pushed her suitcase at him and took hold of his arm. 'Eileen visited me this morning,' she said, when they were walking out of the station. 'Why don't you go and see her one evening when you're in London?'

'Is that a joke?' he asked. 'Because it's not funny.' He was looking around the car park for Angela and the car.

A cruel smile pulled at the corners of Mrs Hathall's mouth. 'Your wife's not here,' she said.

'It doesn't matter,' said Robert. 'It's not far to walk.'

It was unusual for him to be so calm, she thought. Usually he became angry when his mother was rude about Angela. Then they would have an argument. But not today.

It was a beautiful September evening. The sun was warm, and the gardens were bright with the last flowers of summer. But Mrs Hathall noticed none of this. She was thinking about Angela – the woman who broke up a happy marriage.

They turned into Wool Lane and walked past a large house. 'That looks nice,' said Mrs Hathall.

'It's the only other house in the lane,' said Robert. 'A woman called Lake lives there. She's a widow[10].' He looked worried. 'I can't understand what's happened to Angela. I'm sorry about this, Mother. I really am sorry.'

Mrs Hathall was so surprised to hear her son say sorry for something, that she could not think of an answer.

After a minute or two, they came to Robert's cottage[11]. Mrs Hathall was disappointed to see that it was a pleasant old house with brown bricks. Robert unlocked the front door.

'Angela, we're here!' he called.

Mrs Hathall followed him into the living room – and was surprised. Where were the dirty tea-cups and the clothes across the chairs? Where was the dust on the furniture, the dirty windows? She had expected to see all of these things, but the place was amazingly *clean*.

'Where *is* Angela?' said Robert. 'I'm going out to the garage to look for the car. Go on upstairs, Mother. Your bedroom is the big room at the back.'

Murder!

Mrs Hathall climbed the stairs, checking for dust. There was none. And her bedroom was as clean as the rest of the house. Disappointed, she went into the bathroom where there were clean towels and new soap. She washed her hands and came out again. The door to the main bedroom was half-open and Mrs Hathall looked inside.

A girl lay face-down on the bed. Mrs Hathall smiled coldly. Robert's wife was asleep, perhaps drunk. She was wearing shoes, old blue jeans and a red shirt. They were the same clothes that she had worn when they met at Earl's Court. Mrs Hathall remembered Eileen's pretty afternoon dresses. Eileen only slept in the afternoon when she was ill.

She walked across to the bed and looked down at the girl. She put a hand on the girl's shoulder to shake it. Then she stopped. The girl's neck was cold, and there was an ugly purple mark on it.

She was dead.

Mrs Hathall's heart began to beat faster, but she did not scream. She felt only shock, nothing else. Slowly, she walked out of the room and down the stairs.

Robert was waiting at the bottom. She put a hand on his arm.

'There's been an accident,' she said. 'It – it's too late to do anything. Your wife's dead.' She repeated the words because he did not seem to hear them. 'Angela's dead, Robert.'

He did not speak, but walked quickly past her and up the stairs.

She waited. She was shaking now.

Then he called out from above. His voice was quite calm. 'Phone the police, Mother. Tell them what's happened.'

Chief Inspector Reginald Wexford was looking at the dead woman's passport. On the table next to him were her driving licence, purse and other things from her handbag. He and Inspector Burden had arrived at Bury Cottage at 8pm. It was now nearly midnight. Other policemen were upstairs. They were looking for fingerprints[12] and for other clues. It was a big house. There were five large rooms as well as the kitchen and bathroom.

The passport of Angela Margaret Hathall was three years old. It had never been used. Wexford saw that she was thirty-two years old, and born in Melbourne, Australia. After a minute, he moved away from the table and sat down.

'Your wife lived here alone during the week, Mr Hathall. Is that right?' he asked the man sitting in the armchair.

Robert Hathall was a tall man, but thin and with a pale unhealthy look. His black hair was thinning and dry. His mother sat in a straight-backed chair, watching him. There was no kindness or sympathy[13] in her eyes.

Hathall nodded. 'I was working in Toxborough. But in July I got a job in London. I couldn't travel up and down every day. I've been living with my mother during the week. I come home at weekends.'

'You and your mother arrived here at seven-thirty this evening?' asked Wexford.

'Seven-twenty,' said Mrs Hathall, speaking for the first time.

'When did you last see your wife, Mr Hathall?'

'Sunday night,' said Hathall. 'Angela drove me to the railway station. I phoned her every day. I phoned her at lunchtime today. She – she was all right.' He put his head in his hands. 'Who – who could do this? Who would want to kill ... *Angela*?'

The words sounded false to Wexford. Like something from a television film.

'Were you at work all day?' he asked.

'Yes,' said Hathall. He looked up. 'I work at Marcus Flower, Public Relations Consultants, on Half Moon Street. I'm an accountant[14]. You can check with them. I was there all day.' He put his head in his hands again and began to cry loudly.

Wexford watched him silently. Why did he feel no sympathy for this man? Was there really something false about Hathall's behaviour? He waited until the man looked up before he spoke again.

'Your car is missing?' he said.

'It wasn't in the garage when I got home,' said Hathall.

There were no tears on his face. 'But would the son of that hard-faced woman really be able to cry?' Wexford thought.

'Sergeant Martin will get the car's description and number from you in a minute,' he said. 'Try and get some sleep. I'll talk to you again in the morning.'

———

'Where's the garage?' Wexford asked when they were outside.

'It must be at the back,' said Burden.

The two men went outside. 'You can't see it from the lane,'

Wexford said, when they found it. 'She could bring someone here, put the car in the garage and nobody would see her. Then they could go into the house through the back door.' He looked across the moonlit fields. 'The nearest house is that place up by the Stowerton Road. The only other one is Wool Farm, half a mile away.'

They went back to the lane and Wexford walked towards his car. 'I'll see you in the morning, Mike,' he said to Burden. 'It's going to be a busy weekend.'

Wexford's house was to the north of Kingsmarkham. His wife, Dora, was sitting in bed reading when he got there. He gave her a kiss and started to undress.

'What do you know about the people at Bury Cottage in Wool Lane?' he asked her. 'A man called Hathall lives there. His wife was strangled[15] this afternoon.'

After thirty years of marriage to a policeman, Dora Wexford wasn't shocked to hear this. 'Oh, dear,' she said. 'How terrible.' She thought for a moment. 'The only person that I've met from Wool Lane is Mrs Lake. She's a widow. She's very pretty, and she likes men.'

Before he went to sleep, Wexford thought about Angela Hathall. Did she go out in the car, meet a man and bring him back to the cottage? Maybe the man wanted to sleep with her but she didn't want to sleep with him. So he killed her and drove away in her car.

Then Wexford began to think about happier things – his grandchildren, a recent holiday.

He was soon asleep.

2
An Angry Man

Wexford arrived at Bury Cottage at nine o'clock on Saturday morning. Robert Hathall looked better after his night's sleep. But he became angry at Wexford's first question.

'Did your wife sometimes give lifts in her car to strangers?' the chief inspector asked.

'Do you think that my wife took strange men home with her?' said Hathall, angrily. 'She wasn't like that!'

'I don't think anything, Mr Hathall,' said Wexford. 'But I do need to know as much as I can about your wife.'

'A man must have got into the cottage,' said Hathall. 'He – he must have left fingerprints, hairs, footprints. I've read about these things.'

'If a stranger came here yesterday afternoon – ,' Wexford began.

'Of course it was a *stranger*!' said Hathall. 'He got in and – and afterwards he stole my car. Have you found it yet?'

'I don't know, Mr Hathall,' Wexford replied, very coldly and very calmly. 'I haven't had time to speak to my officers. Now, please answer my question. Then I'll leave you for a time and go and talk to your mother.'

'My mother knows nothing about it,' said Hathall. 'She never came here before last night.'

'Answer my question, Mr Hathall.'

'No, Angela did not give lifts to people!' shouted Hathall. 'She was much too shy and nervous.'

He put his face in his hands again. He was shaking. Wexford watched him but said nothing. Then the chief inspector walked through to the kitchen. Mrs Hathall was washing dishes. After a moment she turned and dried her hands on a towel.

'Your son says that your daughter-in-law was shy and nervous,' said Wexford. 'Why was that?'

'I don't know,' said Mrs Hathall. 'I only saw her once.'

'But your son and his wife had been married for three years,' said Wexford.

Mrs Hathall turned away and began drying the dishes. She dried every cup and plate in silence and put them away. At last she looked at him again.

'Your daughter-in-law has been murdered, Mrs Hathall,' said Wexford. 'I have to ask you some questions.'

'I know that she was murdered,' said Mrs Hathall. 'I found her.'

'Yes, tell me about that,' said Wexford.

She stared at him. 'I didn't want to come here,' she said at last.

'Why did you come?' asked Wexford.

'Because my son wanted Angela and me to be friends,' she said. She made it sound impossible. 'Angela was shy and nervous, was she?' she went on. 'Then it was because she was ashamed[16]. She was ashamed of breaking up a happy marriage. She was ashamed of making my son a poor man.'

'I was asking you about last night,' said Wexford.

'She was supposed to meet us at the station,' Mrs Hathall replied. 'We got here and Robert went to look for her. He called out to her. He looked everywhere downstairs, in the garden and in the garage.'

'Did he go upstairs?'

'No. He told me to take my things up to my bedroom. The door to their bedroom was half-open. I saw her and went in. That's all that I can tell you.'

Then Mrs Hathall walked out of the room and up the stairs.

Wexford went back to speak to Robert Hathall again. Hathall was standing by the window. He was looking closely at

An Angry Man

something on the front page of the *Daily Telegraph* newspaper. He turned towards Wexford.

'I won't ask you anything more now, Mr Hathall,' said Wexford. 'Come down to the police station at about three o'clock.'

Hathall nodded. 'I'm sorry that I was angry earlier,' he said.

'That's all right,' said Wexford. 'Before you come this afternoon, please look through your wife's things. See if there's anything missing.'

When Wexford got to his office in Kingsmarkham police station, he picked up the *Daily Telegraph*. The paragraph that Hathall had been reading so closely was at the bottom of the front page. It said: *Mrs Angela Hathall, 32, was last night found*

An Angry Man

dead at her home in Wool Lane, Kingsmarkham, Sussex. She had been strangled. Police are treating the case[17] as murder.

Wexford thought for some minutes. 'Would I want to read about my wife's murder in the newspaper?' he said to himself. The answer was 'no'.

Burden came into the room. 'Here's that report,' he said. 'I've looked quickly at it.'

'Have we found the car?' asked Wexford.

'No,' said Burden. 'Martin checked with Hathall's company, Marcus Flower. He spoke to Hathall's secretary, Linda Kipling. Hathall was there all day yesterday, except for an hour-and-a-half at lunchtime. He left the office at five-thirty.'

Wexford nodded at the report on his desk. 'Tell me about that.'

Burden sat down. 'First of all, Angela Hathall had been very busy cleaning,' he said. 'There weren't many fingerprints in the house. Only a few of Hathall's prints, and some of his mother's. They probably made them after they came home last night. Angela's prints were on the back door, on the door from the kitchen into the hall, and on her bedroom door. That's all. Perhaps she wore gloves[18] to do her housework. The only other prints were those of one unknown man and one unknown woman. The man's prints were only on the books and on the inside of a bedroom cupboard door. Not Angela's bedroom. There's one print of this other woman. A whole handprint. It's the right hand, and it shows a small L-shaped scar[19] on the forefinger. It was on the edge of the bath.'

'Anything else?'

'There were three long dark hairs on the bathroom floor,' said Burden. 'They're not Angela's.'

'Are they from a man or a woman?'

'It's impossible to know,' said Burden.

'OK, we have to find the car,' said Wexford. 'And we have to find someone who saw her go out or come back in it. Perhaps they saw her with a man. We have to find her friends.'

They went downstairs. Burden stopped to speak to the sergeant at the desk. Wexford went outside.

A woman was coming up the steps to the police station door. When she saw Wexford, she stopped and smiled at him. She wasn't young. Probably not quite fifty. She smiled at him again. It was a smile to make a man's heart beat faster. Wexford held the door open for her.

'Good morning,' she said. 'My name is Nancy Lake. I want to see a policeman. Someone important. Are you important?'

'Yes, I suppose I am,' said Wexford.

She smiled again and looked straight into his eyes.

'No woman has looked at me like that for twenty years or more,' thought Wexford.

She walked past him into the police station. 'I've come to tell you something,' she said. 'I think that I was the last person to see Angela Hathall alive.'

3

Nancy Lake

'Were you a friend of Mrs Hathall's?' asked Wexford.

They were in his office. Nancy Lake was sitting opposite him. Wexford remembered his wife's words about her. *She's very pretty, and she likes men.* 'And I'm sure that men like her,' he thought. Nancy Lake saw that he was looking closely at her, and she seemed to enjoy it.

Nancy Lake

'Oh, *no*,' she said. 'I'm a neighbour. I live in the only other house in the lane. I went to the cottage to pick the plums[20].'

'You went there yesterday to pick plums?' said Wexford.

'I always do. Every year,' said Nancy Lake. 'I always picked them when old Mr Somerset lived there. When the Hathalls came, they said that I could have them. I make them into jam.'

'When did you go there?'

'I phoned Angela at 9am. She seemed quite pleased, and asked me to come at half-past twelve. I picked the plums and she gave me a cup of coffee. I think that she wanted me to see the house. Everything was wonderfully clean.'

'Isn't it usually clean?' asked Wexford.

'No,' said Mrs Lake. 'The last time that I was there, it was very untidy. That was in March. Yesterday, she'd cleaned everything because Robert's mother was coming.'

Wexford nodded. Nancy Lake was quite beautiful, and he was finding it difficult not to stare at her. He was not succeeding, and she knew it.

'Was she expecting someone else to call?' he said.

'No, she said that she was going out in the car.'

'Where was she going?' he asked.

'She didn't say.' Nancy Lake leaned across the desk. Her face was close to Wexford's. 'After I finished my coffee, she seemed to want me to go.'

'What time did you leave?' he asked.

'Just before half-past one. I was only in the house for ten minutes. The rest of the time I was picking plums.'

He wanted to stay close to that pretty face, but he carefully turned his chair away. 'Did you see her leave or return to Bury Cottage?'

For the first time, there was something secretive about her reply. 'No, I – I went to Myringham,' she said. 'I was in Myringham all afternoon and part of the evening.'

Nancy Lake

Wexford waited a moment. Then he said, 'Tell me about Angela Hathall. Were she and Robert happy?'

'Oh, yes,' she replied. 'They had no friends, only each other. They seemed happy with that.'

'Some people say that she was shy and nervous.'

'Really?' Nancy Lake said. 'I'm surprised. She seemed to *enjoy* being on her own a lot. Of course, they were quite poor until he got his new job. He still had to pay money to his first wife.'

Wexford turned round again. 'Mrs Lake, can I see your right hand?'

She put it in his hand. It was warm and smooth, and there was a diamond ring on the middle finger. Wexford held it a moment too long.

'How exciting,' she said, smiling. 'To be holding hands with a policeman.'

Wexford quickly turned her hand over. 'Excuse me,' he said. There was no L-shaped scar on her forefinger. He let the hand drop.

'Is that how you check for fingerprints?' she said, still smiling.

'No, it isn't,' he said. He didn't explain. 'Did Angela Hathall have a cleaner?'

'No, I don't think so.' She was silent for a moment. Then she said, 'Can I do anything else for you, Mr Wexford?'

'No, thank you,' he said. 'But I may want to talk to you again, Mrs Lake.'

'Oh, I hope that you do,' she said. She got up and moved towards the window. Wexford stood up. He was standing close to her. She put a hand on his arm.

'Goodbye, Mr Wexford. You must come to tea quite soon. I'll give you some plum jam.'

After Nancy Lake left, he stood by the window and watched her cross the road. Suddenly, she turned and looked back at him. She waved her hand, and he waved his.

'Like old friends,' he thought. Then he went to find Burden.

———

The Carousel Café was opposite the police station. Burden was sitting at their usual corner table. Wexford sat opposite him.

'Angela Hathall went out,' he told Burden, after they had ordered their food. 'She told Mrs Lake that she was going out in the car.'

'The woman with the L-shaped scar?' asked Burden.

'Not Mrs Lake,' said Wexford. 'And she says that Angela didn't have any friends, or a cleaner. Angela cleaned the place because her mother-in-law was coming. But it's strange that she wiped everything clean again before she went out in the car. Mrs Lake had coffee with her about one o'clock, but Mrs Lake's fingerprints aren't in the cottage.'

Their food arrived and they ate in silence. When they were drinking their coffee, Wexford said, 'Hathall behaved very strangely when they got into the house last night.'

'Strangely?' said Burden. 'How?'

'Hathall and his wife had been married for three years,' Wexford explained. 'During that time his mother only met Angela once. There were some angry words – something to do with Angela breaking up Robert's first marriage. They never saw each other after that. But Robert persuaded[21] his mother to come for the weekend. Angela was supposed to meet them at the railway station, but she didn't arrive. Hathall says that she was shy and nervous.'

'Frightened about meeting her mother-in-law,' said Burden.

'Right,' said Wexford. 'But what happened when Hathall got to Bury Cottage? He couldn't find Angela. Now where was his nervous, shy wife most likely to be?'

'In her bedroom,' said Burden.

'Right. But Hathall looked for her *downstairs* and in the garden. He never went upstairs at all. *He sent his mother* upstairs, and went off to the garage. That, Mike, is very strange.'

Burden nodded. 'Drink your coffee,' he said. 'Hathall is coming in at three o'clock. Maybe he'll give you an answer.'

4
Questions About Fingerprints

Wexford pretended to look at Hathall's list of the jewellery[22] that was missing – a bracelet, two rings and a necklace. But he was really watching Hathall. The man seemed angry.

'What do you think happened yesterday afternoon, Mr Hathall?' asked Wexford.

'Why are you asking *me* that?' said Hathall.

'Would anyone be likely to come and see her?' asked Wexford. 'Would she bring someone home?'

'Listen, somebody got into the house to steal from us,' said Hathall. 'He took the things on that list. When my wife tried to stop him, he – he killed her.'

'The person who came into your house wiped the place clean of a large number of fingerprints,' said Wexford. 'A thief[23] wouldn't need to do that. He would wear gloves. And the things on this list are worth about fifty pounds. A thief wouldn't strangle your wife for fifty pounds. Would he hit her? Perhaps. Would he strangle her? No. Who visited your house? What friends called to see your wife?'

'We had no friends,' said Hathall. 'You need money to make friends in a place like Kingsmarkham. When we came here, we didn't have enough money to join clubs or have parties. Angela often saw nobody from Sunday night until Friday night.' He looked straight at Wexford. 'Perhaps I should tell you a bit about myself. You'll understand better.'

Wexford nodded. 'Go on, Mr Hathall.'

'My first marriage wasn't happy.' said Hathall. 'My mother thinks that it was, but she's wrong. I got married seventeen years ago. Two years later I knew that I'd made a mistake. But Eileen and I had a daughter by then, so I stayed with my wife.'

Questions About Fingerprints

'How did you meet Angela?' asked Wexford.

'It was at an office party at Craig and Butler, the firm of accountants in Gray's Inn Road,' Hathall explained. 'I was working there. Angela and I fell in love. I asked Eileen for a divorce – I did not want to be married to her any more – but she refused[24]. She was very angry and said some terrible things. Our daughter, Rosemary, was eleven. Eileen used her and my mother to try and make me stay. But I couldn't.'

'That was five years ago?'

'Yes,' replied Hathall. 'I left home and went to live with Angela. She had a room in Earl's Court. She was working at the library of the National Archaeologists' League. Eileen started to come to my office and to Angela's workplace. She shouted and screamed at us. I asked her again and again for a divorce. Angela had a good job and I had some money at that time. At last, Eileen agreed to the divorce. But by then, Craig and Butler had sacked[25] me because of Eileen's shouting-and-screaming visits to the office. It was wrong of them, but they did it. Then Angela had to leave the library because she was ill with stress[26].'

'What did you do?' asked Wexford.

'I got a part-time job as an accountant with Kidd and Company of Toxborough. They make toys. Angela and I got a room near there. We had almost no money, and Angela was too ill to work. After the divorce, Eileen had my house and my daughter. She was also getting most of my money. Then we had a bit of luck. Angela has a cousin near here. His name is Mark Somerset, and he let us live in Bury Cottage. It had belonged to his father. We had to pay him rent – it didn't matter that he was Angela's cousin. That was three years ago.'

'Did Mr Somerset ever visit you at Bury Cottage?' asked Wexford.

'Never,' said Hathall. 'He showed us the place the first day. After that, we only saw him once. It was on the street in

'Eileen started to come to my office and to Angela's workplace.
She shouted and screamed at us.'

Myringham. He never came to the cottage again. He didn't seem to like Angela.'

'And your mother didn't like Angela,' said Wexford.

'My mother loves Eileen like a daughter,' said Hathall. 'She believes that Angela stole me from her.'

'They only met once. Is that right?' said Wexford.

'I persuaded my mother to come to Earl's Court and meet Angela. It was a mistake,' replied Hathall. 'She didn't like the way Angela was dressed. She was wearing those same jeans and that red shirt. And when Angela said something horrible about Eileen, my mother walked out of the house. After that, she refused to visit us.'

'But you've been staying with her during the week.'

'Yes,' said Hathall. 'When I got this job with Marcus Flower, I decided to stay week-nights with my mother. She lives in Balham, so it wasn't far to go from Victoria Station. Angela and I were looking for a flat to buy in London. Since July, I'd had time to talk to my mother about Angela. It took me eight weeks to persuade her to come here for the weekend.'

'How did you feel when your wife didn't meet you at the station?' asked Wexford.

Hathall was silent for a moment. Then he said, 'I guessed that she was too nervous to come.'

'What did you do at the house?'

'I called out to Angela,' said Hathall. 'When she didn't answer, I looked for her downstairs. Then I went out into the garden. I told my mother to go upstairs. Then I went to look in the garage for the car.'

'You didn't look upstairs.'

'Not at first.'

'Her bedroom would be the most likely place for a nervous woman to go to,' said Wexford. 'Don't you agree? But you didn't go there. You went to the garage and sent your mother upstairs.'

Questions About Fingerprints

'I suppose I thought, "Angela didn't answer when I called, so she's not in the house." Yes, I did think that.' Hathall paused. Then he said, 'Have you had the forensic report yet?'

'Not yet, Mr Hathall,' said Wexford. He was surprised by the question.

'What about the fingerprints? Any clues there?' asked Hathall.

'Very few.'

'It all seems very slow,' said Hathall. 'Please tell me when you know anything. I'd like to know about the forensic report.'

'I'll call and see you tomorrow, Mr Hathall,' said Wexford.

A few moments later, Hathall left the office.

―――

'She was strangled with a necklace,' said Burden.

Wexford looked up from the report in front of him. 'It could be the one on Hathall's list,' he said. 'Time of death, between 1.30pm and 3.30pm. Mrs Lake left her at 1.30pm.'

'What did Hathall say to you?' asked Burden.

Wexford told him of the conversation. 'It's all beginning to look very strange,' he finished. 'I know that Hathall didn't kill her. When she died, he was at work. But why didn't he go upstairs? Why is he angry and not shocked by his wife's murder? And why is he asking about fingerprints?'

'Mrs Lake's and Angela's prints weren't in the living room,' said Burden. 'The killer must have wiped everything clean after the murder. So was it *planned?*'

'Probably,' said Wexford. 'And you're right. I don't believe that Angela cleaned the living room after Mrs Lake left. She wasn't *that* nervous.'

'But the killer left prints on the inside of a cupboard door,' said Burden. 'A cupboard that was never used.'

'I think those prints belonged to a Mr Mark Somerset, the owner of Bury Cottage,' said Wexford. 'Let's find out where he lives in Myringham, then go and see him.'

5
Mark Somerset

Myringham was fifteen miles from Kingsmarkham. Mark Somerset lived in one of the houses by the river. He was in his fifties, but he looked younger. He was slim and healthy-looking, and he wore black jeans and a T-shirt.

'Come in, but be as quiet as you can,' he said. 'My wife only came out of hospital this morning. She's sleeping.'

'Was she in hospital for anything serious?' asked Burden.

'She's been ill for years,' said Somerset, with a sad smile. 'But you haven't come to talk about that. Let's go into the living room.'

There were glass doors at one end of the room. Outside was a small garden. A low table stood in front of the doors. There was a bottle of wine on the table.

'I teach sport at the University of the South, here in Myringham,' said Somerset. 'On Saturday nights I have a glass of wine. Will you have some with me?'

The two policemen accepted the wine. Then Wexford spoke about fingerprints.

Somerset smiled. 'You can take mine,' he said. 'I suppose you found the prints of some unknown mystery man in the cottage. I haven't been there for three years, but I expect they're mine.'

'Tell me about your cousin,' said Wexford.

'Angela?' Somerset replied. 'I first met her about five years ago, after she arrived from Australia. She was the daughter of my father's dead brother. I and my father were her only family in this country. She hadn't met Robert at that time. After she met him she didn't come here again. I wrote to tell her about my father's death, but she didn't reply to my letter. I heard from her again when she and Robert were going to get married. They wanted to live at Bury Cottage.'

'And you let them have it,' said Wexford.

'Yes,' said Somerset. 'I agreed to let them have it for five pounds a week.'

'That's a very low rent, Mr Somerset,' said Wexford.

'I was sorry for them. She told me that they had very little money,' said Somerset. 'And she was my cousin. But I wasn't happy when Angela sent me her electricity bill to pay. That wasn't part of the agreement. I asked her to come here and talk about it.'

'Did she come?'

'Yes, she came and told me that they were very poor. I suggested that she got a job. She told me that she was ill from stress, but I think she was just lazy. She told me that I was mean[27]. Then she walked out of the house. I didn't see either of them again until about eighteen months ago. I was with a friend in Pomfret. We were passing a very expensive restaurant, and I saw them inside, eating. They didn't see me.

'We met again only once more,' he went on. 'Last April, in Myringham. They were shopping and were carrying a lot of parcels[28]. I never saw Angela again, but she wrote to me a month ago. She said they planned to leave the cottage as soon as they found a place in London. I'm sorry she's dead, but I can't say that I liked her.'

'You've been very helpful, Mr Somerset,' said Wexford. 'One more thing. What were you doing yesterday afternoon?'

'I was here alone,' said Somerset, quickly. 'I was getting things ready for my wife's return from hospital.' He nodded towards Wexford's glass. 'Would you like some more wine?'

'No, thank you,' said Wexford. Had the man's reply been almost *too quick*?

When they were leaving the house, a woman's voice called from upstairs. 'Marky, Marky, where are you?'

'We were passing a very expensive restaurant,
and I saw them inside, eating.'

Somerset went to the bottom of the stairs. 'I'm coming!' he called.

Wexford and Burden said goodnight quickly, and left.

In the morning, Wexford returned to Bury Cottage. Mrs Hathall let him in.

'My son's still asleep,' she said.

She took him into the living room and told him to wait there. She didn't offer him tea or coffee.

'Did Robert's first wife ever come here?' asked Wexford.

'Certainly not!' she replied.

'Did Rosemary, your grand-daughter?'

'Rosemary came once, and once was enough,' said Mrs Hathall. 'Anyway, she's too busy with schoolwork to come.'

'Will you give me Mrs Eileen Hathall's address, please?' asked Wexford.

Mrs Hathall's face went bright red. 'No, I won't! Find it yourself!' she said, and she walked out of the room.

Wexford began to look around. Most of the furniture had belonged to Mark Somerset's father, he guessed. There was a bookcase by the window. Most of the books were probably also his father's but some clearly belonged to the Hathalls. There were six books about murder-mysteries, two or three books about archaeology and two large, expensive-looking books.

Wexford took down one of these. It had pictures of very old Egyptian jewellery. Inside the cover were the words: 'Property of the National Archaeologists' League'. 'Stolen, of course, by Angela,' Wexford thought. He took down the second of the two expensive books. Its title was *Of Men and Angels, A Study of Ancient British Language*. Wexford looked inside. There were chapters on Welsh, Scottish, Gaelic[29] and Cornish. He was surprised. It was a subject that even he would find difficult to read and understand.

He was holding the book when Hathall came into the room.

He saw the man's eyes look at it, then look away quickly.

'Are you a student of Celtic languages, Mr Hathall?' asked Wexford.

'No. It was Angela's book,' said Hathall. 'She's had it for years.'

'That's strange, because it was only published this year. But it doesn't matter.' Wexford smiled. 'We've found your car. It was in a street near Wood Green station in London. Do you know that area?'

'I've never been there,' said Hathall. Again, he looked at the book which Wexford was holding. 'When can I have my car back?'

'In two or three days,' said Wexford.

'When you've looked for those fingerprints that you're always talking about?' said Hathall.

'Am I, Mr Hathall? Or are they something that you *want me* to talk about?' replied Wexford. 'You might like to know that your wife died very quickly. In no more than fifteen seconds.'

He waited for the other man to say something, but Hathall continued to look at the book. Wexford closed it.

'Can I borrow this for a few days?' he asked.

Hathall nodded but said nothing.

6

A Shock for Hathall

The inquest was on Tuesday morning. The verdict was 'murder by person or persons unknown'. Afterwards, Wexford saw Nancy Lake go to speak to Robert Hathall and his mother. Hathall said something to Mrs Lake. Then he walked away quickly.

A Shock for Hathall

Some moments later, Wexford was walking towards his office. A car stopped next to him.

'Are you very busy, Chief Inspector?' It was Nancy Lake.

'Why do you ask, Mrs Lake?' said Wexford.

'It's not because I have any interesting clues to give you,' she replied. She put a hand out of the car window and touched his arm. 'I have a table for two booked at the Peacock Restaurant in Pomfret. But my friend can't come. Would *you* like to have lunch with me instead?' She smiled at him.

Wexford was shocked. This rich and pretty woman was flirting[30] with him!

'I also have a table booked for lunch,' he said. 'At the Carousel Café. And, yes, I am very busy.'

He walked away quickly and up to his office. Was he stupid to refuse her invitation? He decided not to think about it.

He began reading the report about Robert Hathall's car. It had been found in a street near Alexandra Park. It was empty, except for a couple of maps and a pen. It had been wiped clean, inside and out. There were just two of Angela's hairs on the driving seat.

Sergeant Martin had nothing new to tell him. Nobody saw Angela go out or come home on Friday afternoon. Nobody had come to the police station to say that they were a friend of Angela's.

Wexford went alone to the Carousel Café for lunch.

Wexford had been sitting at his corner table for about five minutes. Suddenly a hand touched his shoulder. He turned slowly.

'Mrs Lake,' he said coolly.

She sat down opposite him.

'What will you eat?' he asked.

'Nothing. I'll just have a cup of coffee,' she replied with a smile.

His food arrived and he said to the waiter, 'Bring a coffee for the lady, please.'

Nancy Lake was silent while Wexford was eating. Then she said, 'I'm sad, Mr Wexford. Things aren't going well for me.'

He was very surprised. 'Do you want to tell me about it?' he asked.

'I don't know,' she said. 'No, I don't think so. A person can have secrets.'

'That's true, sometimes,' said Wexford.

Then she said, 'Is it very wrong to want someone to die?'

The question surprised him. It was so surprising that Wexford pushed his plate away and stared at her.

'It's all right to *want* it,' he answered. 'Most of us want it sometimes. Happily, most of us do nothing about it.'

She nodded. 'I'm sorry that I spoke about it,' she said quickly. 'It was stupid. You're a clever man. You probably know the person that I'm talking about.'

He didn't answer.

'Let's talk about something else,' she said.

They did. But afterwards he could not remember their conversation. He only knew that it had been very enjoyable. Too enjoyable. He was a married man, and he felt bad. He decided that he would not see her again.

———

Wexford had forgotten about the book of Celtic languages. Hathall asked for it back as soon as the policeman arrived at Bury Cottage.

'Of course,' said Wexford. 'I'll send it over to you.'

'And I need my car,' said Hathall.

'You can have that, too.'

'Did you find any clues in it?'

'No,' said Wexford. 'The person who killed your wife was very clever. *Very* clever.' He watched the other man carefully. Hathall looked ... *satisfied*[31]. 'He wore gloves to drive your

A Shock for Hathall

car,' Wexford went on. 'Then he washed it. Nobody saw him driving it or parking it. At the moment, we have very few clues to work on. But we did find a man's fingerprints in this house. We know now that they were Mark Somerset's prints.'

Hathall suddenly seemed more relaxed and friendly. 'So, the only prints you found were cousin Mark's,' he said.

'I didn't say that, Mr Hathall,' said Wexford. 'We also found a woman's handprint in your bathroom. It's the print of her right hand, and there's an L-shaped scar on her forefinger.'

Hathall did not move. He said nothing, but all the colour left his face. Shock had come to him at last. Wexford was excited to see this, but he spoke calmly.

'Perhaps you know this person, Mr Hathall?'

Hathall seemed to have trouble breathing. He shook his head slowly.

'Are you sure, Mr Hathall?' asked Wexford. 'An L-shaped scar on their forefinger?'

'On the bath?' said Hathall.

'Yes,' said Wexford. 'You can guess the person who – '

'No!' said Hathall. His voice was weak. 'No, I don't know.'

The worst of the shock had passed. Some colour was returning to Hathall's face.

'You've been very interested in fingerprints all through this investigation, Mr Hathall,' said Wexford. 'I think that you expected us to find this print. I think you know something, but you're not telling me. I must tell you that it's a crime to keep important information from the police.'

'Don't threaten[32] me!' said Hathall.

'You would be sensible to tell me anything that you can,' said Wexford.

Hathall said nothing. Wexford waited a moment or two, then he walked out of the house. He was sure Hathall knew the woman with the L-shaped scar.

He was also sure that Hathall had killed his wife.

7
A Very Small Fraud[33]

Chief Superintendent Howard Fortune, of Kenbourne Vale Criminal Investigation Department, was Wexford's nephew. Wexford had once helped Howard with a murder case. Howard and his wife, Denise, were always kind and welcoming to Wexford and Dora. They had enjoyed several Christmases together.

'Give me an hour to get ready,' Dora said to Wexford, when he suggested visiting them for a few days.

Wexford made a phone call, and the visit was arranged quickly and easily. He and Dora arrived at the Fortunes' London house just after seven o'clock that evening.

The next morning, Wexford went up to the West End and the offices of Marcus Flower. He discovered that Marcus Flower was two people – Jason Marcus and Stephen Flower. The two men said that they were sorry about 'poor old Robert's wife'.

Wexford refused a cup of black coffee. Then he said, 'I've really come to talk to Linda Kipling – Mr Hathall's secretary.'

Jason Marcus took him to her and left them. Linda looked a little like a shop-window dummy[34] in a very expensive dress shop. She didn't seem like a real person.

'Robert phoned his wife every day at lunchtime,' she said, looking at her green fingernails.

'Do you think that it was a happy marriage?' asked Wexford.

'I don't know,' said Linda. 'He never spoke about it.'

'Tell me about last Friday,' said Wexford. 'What was he like?'

'Just the same,' she replied. 'He got in a bit before ten o'clock and he was here all morning. He phoned his wife just before one o'clock. Then he went out to lunch with Jason. He was back by half-past two. Then he left at half-past five to go and meet his mother.'

'Did he ever get phone calls here from women or a woman that wasn't his wife?' Wexford asked.

'His wife never phoned *him*,' she said. After a moment, she gave a little laugh. 'Oh, you mean a girlfriend? No! Nobody ever phoned him.'

'Did Mr Hathall have a special friendship with any girl here?' asked Wexford.

'Do you mean, was he *sleeping* with anyone who worked here?'

'Well, he was a lonely man,' replied Wexford, 'separated from his wife all week. There are five girls here, and …'

'June and Liz are married,' said Linda. 'Clare is soon to marry Jason, and Suzanne is Lord Carthew's daughter.'

'Would that stop her from sleeping with a man?' asked Wexford.

'It would stop her from sleeping with someone like Robert Hathall,' she answered coldly. 'And that's true for all of us!'

Wexford said good morning to her and walked out. In Piccadilly, he telephoned Craig and Butler, Accountants, of Gray's Inn Road. Craig and Butler was the firm where Hathall worked when he first met Angela. Wexford arranged to see Mr Butler at three o'clock that afternoon.

Next, he went to The National Archaeologists' League Library in Trident Place. There, a girl took him to the office of Miss Marie Marcovitch, the chief librarian. She was a little woman in her late sixties. She asked Wexford to sit down. She did not seem surprised that he had come to ask her about a murder case.

'Angela Hathall left here before her marriage,' said Wexford. 'But how would you describe her? Was she nervous? Or shy?'

'Well, she was quiet,' said Miss Marcovitch. 'She was quite ordinary. She came to work here about five years ago.'

'Was she interested in Celtic languages?' asked Wexford.

Miss Marcovitch looked surprised. 'I don't think that she was. I don't know.'

'It doesn't matter,' said Wexford. 'Please go on.'

'Angela was off sick[35] quite a lot. And she was not good with money. She complained[36] that her pay was never enough. I'm told by others here that she often borrowed small amounts of money from them.'

'And she worked here for some months before she met Mr Hathall?' asked Wexford.

'I'm not sure when she met him,' said Miss Marcovitch.

'First of all she was friendly with a man called Mr Craig. He doesn't work here now. I never met Mr Hathall.'

'But you met the first Mrs Hathall? Mrs Eileen Hathall?'

'I – I don't like to speak badly about other people, but …' She gave a little smile. 'Well, yes, I was in the library when she first came in. This is a very quiet place, Mr Wexford. So I was very angry when this woman came running in and began shouting "You're stealing my husband!" at Angela. It was very embarrassing for everyone here. I asked Mr Craig to take the woman out as quietly as he could. Then I took Angela to my office. When she was calm, I told her that this must not happen again.'

'Did it?' asked Wexford.

'No,' replied Miss Marcovitch. 'But soon after, Angela left her job here. She said that her doctor told her to do this because she was stressed.'

They were silent for some moments. Then Wexford said, 'There's something more that you can tell me. Am I right, Miss Marcovitch?'

She smiled. 'You're very clever, Mr Wexford. Yes, there is one more thing. I've never told anyone about this, but I'll tell you. People who use the library can keep books for one month. But we don't ask them to pay anything when they bring them back late. New people are often happily surprised when they discover this.

'About three years ago, a man brought in three books that were six weeks late. I was helping at the desk on that day. It was several months after Angela left us. The man started to give me some money. I told him that it wasn't necessary. Then he said, "I kept books longer than a month once before. The young lady working here asked me for one pound twenty pence."'

Miss Marcovitch paused and looked at Wexford. Then she said,

'I immediately began questioning the other girls here. They told me that several other people had tried to pay something for late-returned books.'

'And you think that the "young lady" was Angela?'

'Yes, I do,' said Miss Marcovitch. 'But I didn't do anything about it. It was a very small fraud.'

8
Eileen Hathall

It was a very small fraud …

Wexford had not expected it. 'It's probably nothing to do with the murder,' he said to himself, when he left the library.

He took an underground train to Chancery Lane. The offices of Craig and Butler were on the third floor of an old building. Before he went there, Wexford had lunch in a nearby café. At one minute to three o'clock, he was taken to the office of Mr William Butler. Butler was about the same age as Miss Marcovitch, and the room was as quiet as the library. There was a picture of an old man on one wall.

'That's my retired[37] partner, Mr Craig,' said William Butler.

'Did his son introduce Robert and Angela Hathall?' said Wexford.

'No, it was his nephew,' said Butler. 'Jonathan Craig. He worked at the archaeologists' place. He introduced Robert to Angela at my partner's retirement party.'

'Did you meet Angela there?'

'It was the only time I did meet her. I met the first Mrs Hathall, too.' Butler laughed. 'She came here to see Robert. He locked himself in his office! Another time she sat on the stairs all day waiting for him. He locked himself in his office again and never went out all night. The next day she came back and screamed and shouted at me. She wanted him to go back to her and her daughter.'

'And because of this, you sacked him?' asked Wexford.

'No! Did he tell you that? It's not true. I only told Robert to manage his private life better. He got angry and said that he was leaving. I tried to persuade him to stay, but he wouldn't listen.'

'Was Robert Hathall the kind of man who would break the law[38]?' asked Wexford.

'Not at all!' said Butler. 'He didn't always tell the truth, but he was honest[39]. Do you think that he killed Angela?'

'I can't say anything about that, Mr Butler,' said Wexford.

'No, sorry, it was a silly question,' said Butler. 'I thought that he was going to murder his first wife. I'll never forget her visit here as long as I live!'

———

Howard Fortune was tall and thin with light grey-blue eyes. He and Wexford sat in Howard's study.

'I believe that Hathall arranged the killing of Angela,' said Wexford. 'And that somebody helped him.'

'You mean another woman?' said Howard. 'A lover?'

'Yes,' said Wexford.

'So this girlfriend came to the cottage in the afternoon?'

'Or Angela brought her there.'

'And the girl strangled Angela with a necklace,' said Howard. 'Then she wiped her fingerprints off everything except the side of the bath. Is that your idea?'

'Yes. Afterwards she drove Robert Hathall's car to London and left it in Wood Green. Perhaps I'll go there tomorrow. Then I'll go to the toy factory in Toxborough. Hathall worked there from the time of his marriage until last July. It's possible that he knew this woman *before* he met Angela. Or that he met her when his marriage was three years old.'

'Perhaps she was just a friend, or the wife of a friend?'

'He doesn't seem to have any friends.'

'Maybe I'll come with you tomorrow,' said Howard.

The phone rang and Howard picked it up. A moment later he gave it to Wexford. It was Burden.

'Good news first,' said the inspector. 'Hathall's car arrived back at Bury Cottage at five minutes past three on that Friday afternoon. A man saw a dark-haired young woman driving it. She was wearing a red shirt. There was a passenger in the car, and the man thinks that it was a woman.'

'Why didn't this man come and tell us earlier?'

'He's been on holiday,' said Burden. 'He knew nothing about the murder until he saw a newspaper today.'

'So that's the good news,' said Wexford. 'What's the bad news?'

Eileen Hathall

'It may not be bad, I don't know. The chief constable wants to see you at three o'clock tomorrow afternoon.'

Wexford put down the phone. 'We can't go to Wood Green tomorrow,' he told Howard. 'I'll have to try and visit Croydon or Toxborough on my way home,' he explained. 'I won't have time for both.'

'Listen, Reg,' said Howard. 'I can drive you to Croydon. I'd like to meet the first Mrs Hathall. We can go to Toxborough on the way to Kingsmarkham. I know that Denise would like Dora to stay here for a bit longer.'

'That would be great,' said Wexford.

Eileen Hathall was about forty years old. Wexford began by asking her about the day of the murder.

'I was at my father's house in Balham until the evening,' she replied quietly and calmly. 'My daughter was on a school trip to France for the day.'

She gave Wexford her father's address in London.

'That's in the next street to your mother-in-law's house,' said Howard.

Suddenly, her calmness disappeared and her face became red.

'Robert and I were children together,' she said. 'We went to the same school, and we saw each other every day. After we got married, we were together every day and night. Until that woman *stole* him from me!'

'When did you last see Robert?' asked Wexford.

'I haven't seen him for three and a half years,' she answered.

'What about Rosemary?'

'After the divorce, he was allowed to see her every two weeks, on a Sunday,' she said. 'I'd send her to his mum and he'd meet her there.'

'Does he still see your daughter?'

'No,' replied Eileen Hathall. 'Robert hurt me badly when he went off with *that* woman. Rosemary saw that. She didn't want to see him. Robert's mum and I agreed with her. He wrote her letters and sent her presents. He wanted to take her away on holiday. He says that he hasn't got any money.' She gave an angry laugh. 'He's got enough when *he* wants to spend it! I want him to buy Rosemary a car for her eighteenth birthday. I'm going to get his mum to ask him.'

Wexford shook hands with her when they left. There was no scar on her forefinger.

'He certainly didn't kill Angela to go back to Eileen,' said Howard, when they were in the car.

'And she and old Mrs Hathall have taught Rosemary to hate him,' said Wexford.

The two men had a quick lunch in a pub in Toxborough. Then they went to visit Kidd and Company toy factory where Hathall worked after leaving Craig and Butler. The manager, Mr Aveney, told them that three hundred people worked at the factory. Most of them were women. There were seven people working in the offices.

'None of the female office staff here now worked here when Mr Hathall was with us,' explained Aveney. 'And he only left us ten weeks ago. Girls change their jobs a lot these days. I've made a list of the girls who *were* here when he was here.'

He gave Wexford a piece of paper with names and addresses on it.

'Thank you,' said Wexford. He had phoned Aveney earlier and asked for this list. 'Was he very friendly with any one girl?' the policeman asked. 'Can you remember?'

'No,' said Aveney. 'He loved his wife. He talked about her all the time.'

Some minutes later, Wexford and Howard said goodbye and went back to the car.

'Not much help really,' said Wexford.

Eileen Hathall

They drove back to Kingsmarkham.

'Mark Somerset met the Hathalls when they were shopping here,' said Wexford.

Soon after, they were out of the town and in country lanes. After a time, Wexford said, 'Turn right here. It's a little road that becomes Wool Lane.'

They passed Wool Farm and saw the sign Wool Lane. It was a very narrow road.

'There's Bury Cottage,' said Wexford.

Howard slowed the car. At that moment, Robert Hathall came out of the cottage. He began to work in the garden.

'That's him,' said Wexford. 'Did you get a good view of him?'

'Yes,' said Howard.

Howard left Wexford at Kingsmarkham police station. He had to drive on to Brighton for a dinner appointment. The chief constable's car was already in the car park. He was early for his appointment with Wexford.

Charles Griswold was a very tall man. He was even taller than Wexford.

'Let me guess,' said Wexford. 'Hathall's been complaining.'

'He sent me a letter,' said Griswold. 'He says that you've been playing games with him. He said you talked about a fingerprint. Then you walked out of the house without waiting for his answer. Have you got any evidence against him?'

'No,' Wexford replied. 'But I've got a very strong feeling that he killed his wife.'

'*Feeling?*' said Griswold. 'We hear too much about feelings these days. Are you saying that he had a person to help him? Have you got any evidence about that person?'

'No, sir, I haven't,' said Wexford. 'Can I see Hathall's letter?'

'No, you can't,' said Griswold. 'And stay away from him. That's an order. I don't want to hear any more about your *feelings*.'

9
Wexford Gets Help

Wexford was angry. Could he still investigate the mystery woman with the L–shaped scar? Burden and Martin could watch Hathall. He could get other men to speak to the girls on Aveney's list. It could be done. It *had* to be done. Hathall was guilty[40], Wexford was sure about that.

He sent the book *Of Men and Angels* back to Hathall. Then he had a lonely weekend at home. He thought about phoning Nancy Lake, but quickly decided to forget the idea.

At the end of the second week after Angela's death, he and Burden talked about the investigation during lunch.

'We don't know that Hathall had a girlfriend,' Burden told him. 'We're only guessing.'

'What about the woman's handprint?' said Wexford. 'And those long dark hairs? And that man who saw a woman with Angela in the car?'

'He *thought* it was a woman,' said Burden. 'We've investigated all the girls on Aveney's list. Most of them don't remember Hathall.'

'What's your idea about it then, Mike?' asked Wexford.

'I'll tell you,' said Burden. 'A man killed Angela. She was lonely and she gave him a lift in her car. She brought him back to the cottage, and he strangled her. Perhaps it was an accident, when he tried to get the necklace off her. Why *should* he leave fingerprints? Why should he touch anything in the house except Angela?'

'What about the woman's print?' said Wexford.

'She could be a driver who asked to use the phone.'

'Why hasn't the woman come to see us?' said Wexford.

'Because she doesn't know the name of the house that she called at,' answered Burden. 'Or the name of the woman who let her in. And her prints aren't on the phone because Angela was still cleaning the place.'

Griswold liked Burden's explanation. Wexford had to agree to a country-wide search for a female car driver, and a thief who had killed for a necklace. They weren't found.

———

The weeks went on and nothing new happened. Then one morning Burden had some new information.

'Hathall's moving from Bury Cottage,' he told Wexford. 'He's going to stay with his mother in Balham. He's talking about getting a flat in Hampstead.'

Wexford Gets Help

For a long time after that, Wexford heard nothing about Hathall. Then one day in the spring, Burden told him Hathall's new address. They were having lunch in the Carousel Café. Wexford stopped eating and waited for Burden to go on.

'You think that Hathall killed Angela to be able to marry this other woman. The handprint woman,' said Burden. 'But she had a scar on her finger. So why didn't Hathall tell her to *wear gloves*? It needed only one print to identify[41] her.'

Wexford didn't say anything. But that night he looked at a map of London. Then he made a phone call.

The Fortunes had come to stay for the weekend. Howard and Wexford walked down Wool Lane and stopped outside Bury Cottage. It was still empty.

'Hathall lives in London now,' Wexford said. 'He's in West Hampstead, in Dartmeet Avenue. Do you know it?'

'Yes, it's between Finchley Road and West End Lane,' said Howard.

'The only woman that he sees is his mother,' said Wexford.

Howard looked surprised. 'Do you have somebody watching him?' he asked.

'Yes,' said Wexford. 'His name's Ginge Matthews, and he lives in Kilburn. I pay him from my own money.'

They began to walk on, away from the cottage.

'What do you hope to find out, Reg?' asked Howard.

Wexford didn't reply at once. They walked past Nancy Lake's house. Her car stood outside the garage.

'Hathall wasn't just frightened when I told him about the handprint,' Wexford said, after a time. 'He also seemed sad. It was because he'd killed Angela to be with this woman. Now he knew that he could never see her again. It would be too dangerous for both of them.

'And after he thought more about it, he wrote that letter to Griswold,' Wexford went on. 'Why? Because he wanted me to stop the investigation. He knows that I know the truth. Now he can't ever marry or be seen with a woman with an L-shaped scar on her forefinger.'

'So what can he do?' asked Howard.

Wexford paused. Then he said, 'They may have decided not to see each other again.'

'But for how long?' said Howard. 'For ever?'

'Maybe,' said Wexford. 'But he may have decided to see her secretly, until they can think of a better idea. Think about it. Why has he chosen north-west London to live? Why not live near his mother and daughter, or his work? He's living in West Hampstead because nobody knows him there. Because he can secretly go out in the evenings to be with *her*. I'm going to try and find her.'

Wexford learned nothing about the woman from Ginge Matthews' reports to him. But he learned a lot about Robert Hathall's life. One of the reports read:

Hathall has a flat in a large house. He has no garage but he leaves his car in the street. He leaves for work at nine o'clock in the morning. He either walks or gets on a bus from West End Green to West Hampstead Underground Station. There he gets on a Bakerloo Line train to Piccadilly. He arrives home again soon after six o'clock in the evening. Several times, I have seen him go out again in his car.

Hathall's flat is on the second floor of the house. When he is home in the evenings, there is always a light in his window. I have only seen him with his mother. Hathall brought her to his flat one Saturday afternoon.

Ginge had no car and no job. But Wexford could only pay him enough to watch Hathall one evening and one Saturday or Sunday every week. Maybe Hathall brought the woman home on one or two of the other evenings.

Then in September, Ginge wrote:

Hathall has sold his car. It is not parked outside. On Thursday, the 10th of September, he arrived home at 6.10pm. At 6.50pm he left his flat and got on a number 28 bus at West End Green.

Did it mean anything? Wexford didn't think that it did. Hathall didn't need a car.

Wexford never wrote to Ginge. He posted Ginge's wages[42] to him. When he wanted to see him, Wexford went to a pub in Kilburn. Ginge was always there between twelve and one o'clock in the afternoon.

'Follow him?' said Ginge. 'On the 28 bus? I don't like it.'

'It'll be OK. He's never seen you, has he?' said Wexford.

'Maybe he has,' said Ginge. 'I don't know.'

Ginge's next report said nothing about buses. But it was interesting.

I've discovered that there are only single rooms for rent at the house.

This surprised Wexford. Why was Hathall renting only one room? Why didn't he buy a flat? Was it because he wasn't going to stay there long? Did he have other things to spend his money on?

'He's paying for *her* rent, too,' said Howard, when Wexford told him.

'Yes,' said Wexford. 'It's good to hear you talk about her, Howard. You believe that there *is* a woman.'

'Somebody made that handprint, Reg.'

The police at Kingsmarkham had stopped searching. Mark Somerset let two Americans rent Bury Cottage. One day the plums were on the trees, the next day they were gone. Did Nancy Lake take them for jam? Wexford never knew. He

Wexford Gets Help

hadn't seen her since the day that Griswold told him to stay away from Hathall.

No more reports came from Ginge for two weeks. Finally Wexford phoned him at the Kilburn pub. 'Hathall is staying in during the evenings that I've watched the house,' Ginge told him. 'I'll watch again tonight, and on Saturday afternoon.'

A report came on Monday. It read:

Hathall did his usual shopping on Saturday. But on Friday evening he walked to the bus stop at West End Green at 7pm. I followed him to the bus stop but not on to the bus.

Another report came a week later. At the end of it, Ginge wrote:

Hathall called at a travel agency on Saturday.

'He went to Sudamerica Tours, Howard,' Wexford told Howard over the phone. 'Ginge didn't follow him in.'

'You're thinking the same thing that I'm thinking,' said Howard.

'Yes,' said Wexford. 'He's going to Brazil or some place that we can't get him. But are Marcus Flower sending him abroad?

Can you find out, Howard? I can't do it.'

'OK,' said Howard. 'I'll phone you tomorrow.'

The *Kingsmarkham Courier* newspaper was on Wexford's desk. He saw a name in the list of deaths on the back page. *Somerset*. He read the paragraph under the name. *On October the 15th, at Church House, Old Myringham, Gwendolen Mary Somerset, much loved wife of Mark Somerset.*

She's been ill for years. Wexford remembered Mark Somerset's words. Had she been a *much loved* wife? Or were those just words for the newspaper?

Howard's phone call came late the next morning.

'Hathall is leaving Marcus Flower,' he told Wexford. 'That's all I could find out. But I've seen him.'

'*What?*' said Wexford. 'Do you mean that you've talked to him?'

'No, I've *seen* him,' replied Howard. 'With a woman. I've seen him with a woman, Reg.'

10

The Necklace

'It was yesterday evening,' said Howard. 'Denise and I were going to a restaurant. I parked the car near Half Moon Street. We were a few minutes early for the restaurant, so I went to look at the offices of Marcus Flower. I'd phoned them earlier in the day. There was a man and a woman outside the offices. The man was Robert Hathall. He seemed to be showing the woman where he worked. She was nice-looking, with short blonde hair. Probably about thirty years old. Of course, I didn't see her hand. After a minute or two, they walked off towards Piccadilly.'

The Necklace

'So they didn't "shake hands for ever" like the poem says,' said Wexford. 'They didn't say goodbye and disappear from each other's lives. They're still together.'

The next day wasn't a working day for Wexford. At 10.30am he got a train from Kingsmarkham to London. He arrived at Victoria Station just before half-past eleven. By twelve o'clock, he was in Kilburn.

Ginge Matthews was surprised to see Wexford. He was sitting at a corner table in the pub. One of his eyes was half-closed, and there was a purple mark round it.

Wexford bought himself a glass of white wine.

'Do you see my eye?' Ginge said when Wexford arrived at the corner table.

'Of course I see it,' said Wexford. 'Who hit you?'

'Hathall!' said Ginge. 'He did it last night, when I was following him to the 28 bus stop.'

'What!' said Wexford. 'So he knows that you're following him?'

'Yes, so I'm not going back there again,' replied Ginge.

'Tell me about this 28 bus. Where does it go?'

Ginge took a drink from his glass. Then he said, 'Golders Green, Child's Hill, Fortune Green, West End Lane, West Hampstead Station, Quex Road, Kilburn High Road …'

'I don't know any of those places,' said Wexford. 'Where does it finish?'

'Wandsworth Bridge.'

Wexford was disappointed. 'That's near Balham,' he said. 'He's only going to see his mother.'

'No, Mr Wexford,' replied Ginge. 'Nobody goes to Balham that way. They'd go to West Hampstead Underground and change trains at Waterloo or the Elephant and Castle.'

'Then he's getting off the bus somewhere else,' said Wexford. 'Is there a pub near the 28 bus stop?'

'There's one opposite. Why?' asked Ginge, nervously.

The Necklace

'I want you to sit in that pub at six-thirty every night for a week,' said Wexford. 'I need to know how often he catches that bus. Will you do that? You don't have to follow him.'

A day or two later, Wexford had a phone call from one of the new people who had just moved to Bury Cottage. The woman had found a necklace in the garden. Wexford was excited, and he immediately drove to Wool Lane. He noticed a 'For Sale' sign outside Nancy Lake's house when he went past. At Bury Cottage, he walked into the garden.

The woman, Mrs Snyder, met him.

'I told Mr Somerset about the necklace, and he told me to phone you,' she said. 'We've been digging[43] up the garden. There was an old cesspit[44] under here. The necklace was in it. When we started digging, we broke the cesspit open. The necklace was inside. I've washed it and put it in the kitchen.'

Wexford took the necklace back to Kingsmarkham police station. It was made of grey metal, in the shape of a snake. But how did it get in an old cesspit?

Wexford phoned Mark Somerset.

'I can explain,' said Somerset. 'The main drainage[45] came to Kingsmarkham twenty years ago. But my father only paid for the toilet waste to go to it. The waste from the bath, the bathroom hand basin and the kitchen sink went on passing into the cesspit.'

'So the killer dropped the necklace into the sink and washed it down with water,' said Wexford. 'Thanks, Mr Somerset. Oh, and I was sorry to hear about your wife's death.'

'Well – er – yes, thanks,' said Somerset.

Wexford saw Griswold the next day. He showed him the necklace.

'Why do you think that this is the weapon?' asked Griswold. 'Perhaps it's been in the cesspit for twenty years.'

'I could ask Hathall about that,' said Wexford.

The Necklace

'He wasn't there when she was killed, remember?'

'His girlfriend was,' said Wexford.

'Where? When? Are you telling me that you've identified a female?'

'Well, no, but – '

'Reg, have you got any more evidence against Hathall?' said Griswold. 'More than you had fourteen months ago?' He was becoming angry.

Wexford couldn't tell Griswold about Ginge Matthews. He couldn't say that Chief Superintendent Fortune had seen Hathall with a woman. He couldn't prove[46] that Hathall had a job waiting for him somewhere in South America.

'No, sir,' Wexford said at last.

'Then nothing's changed,' said Griswold. 'You stay away from Hathall.'

11
The Girl

On Friday, the 8th of November, a report arrived from Ginge. The report said that on the Monday and Wednesday evenings, Hathall had got on the 28 bus just before seven o'clock. The next Monday, Ginge phoned Wexford.

'I've seen him with a woman,' said Ginge, excitedly.

'Where?' asked Wexford.

'I was in the pub yesterday, at about one o'clock,' said Ginge. 'He went past, down West End Lane. A few minutes later, I went to West Hampstead Station. He was waiting for somebody. About twenty people came up the steps from the trains. I didn't want him to see me. I didn't want him to hit my other eye. When I did turn round, he'd gone.

'I went back to West End Lane,' Ginge went on, 'and he was walking along the road. It was raining hard, and he had an umbrella. He and the woman were under it, but I couldn't see her face. I went home after that.'

———

Later, Wexford said to his wife, 'I'm going to take two weeks holiday.'

'In November?' said Dora. 'Well, Malta is very nice at this time of year.'

'So is Chelsea,' said Wexford. 'We'll be going there.'

On the first day of his 'holiday', Wexford got a number 28 bus to West Hampstead. It took almost an hour. He got off at West End Green. Darmeet Avenue was about a quarter of a mile to the east.

'Why did Hathall get a bus for that short distance?' thought Wexford.

He found number 62. It was one of several tall houses with

The Girl

small gardens. He looked up and saw the window of Hathall's room. Then he turned away and walked slowly back to West End Green.

He got on another 28 bus and went to Kilburn. It was almost twelve o'clock, and Ginge was in the pub. But Ginge refused to do any more watching or following. His wife had got a job, he told Wexford. He didn't need the money now. And he had to stay at home and look after the kids.

———

Wexford sat in his car in Dartmeet Avenue every evening. On Monday, Tuesday and Wednesday, he got there at six o'clock. But he never saw Hathall. On Thursday, he didn't get to the avenue until 6.15pm. There was a light in Hathall's window. Wexford watched the house until the light went out. Hathall didn't come out.

'He's gone to bed,' Wexford thought.

On Friday, Dora went shopping with Denise. Wexford went to Eileen Hathall's house. Robert's car was parked outside the garage. It was the car that Ginge thought had been sold.

'He gave his car to Rosemary,' Eileen Hathall explained to him, some minutes later. 'He won't need it now that he's going away.'

'Where is he going, Mrs Hathall?' asked Wexford.

'Brazil,' she said. She did not sound pleased. 'He's leaving the day before Christmas Eve.'

'Has he got a job there?'

'A very good job,' she said. 'Why do you want to know? Do you think that he killed that woman?'

'Do *you*?' he said.

Her face went bright red. 'I wish that he had!' she said.

Wexford drove back to London, and to Dartmeet Avenue that evening. But he did not see Hathall then or the next day.

———

The Girl

It was 12.30pm on Sunday, the 1st of December, and it was raining hard. Wexford was in his car, nearly opposite the station. He could see the entrance clearly, and most of West End Lane. At ten minutes to one, Hathall walked past Wexford's car without turning his head. He went into the station. Wexford heard a train arriving. A few minutes later, people began to come out of the station.

A man put a newspaper over his head and ran to get out of the rain. Three women put up umbrellas, and walked away. Behind them was a man and a woman with their backs to the street. It was Hathall. The man opened a black umbrella, and they both walked away under it.

She wore blue jeans and a white raincoat. Wexford had not seen her face. Suddenly, a taxi came down the road, and Hathall put up his hand to stop it. The two of them got in, and the taxi drove away. It was gone before Wexford could follow it.

He drove to Dartmeet Avenue. The taxi had gone when he arrived at number 62, but there was a light on in Hathall's room. Of course, Hathall would have to put on a light on a dark, wet day like this, thought Wexford.

He went up to the front door and looked at the doorbells. There were no names, only floor numbers. He pushed the first-floor bell and waited. Above his head, a window opened. Wexford stepped back and looked up into Hathall's face.

At first, Hathall looked surprised, then angry. 'I'll come down and let you in,' he said coldly.

A minute later, Wexford was following him up the stairs. Hathall was quite calm and relaxed now.

'I'd like to meet the lady who came here in a taxi,' said Wexford.

Hathall did not answer. He pushed open the door of his room. Wexford walked in. The room was very small. There was a cupboard, a narrow bed, some chairs, a sink and a cooker.

The Girl

The girl stood beside the sink. She was young, with thick black hair.

'This is the "lady" that you wanted to meet,' said Hathall. He was almost laughing. 'My daughter, Rosemary.'

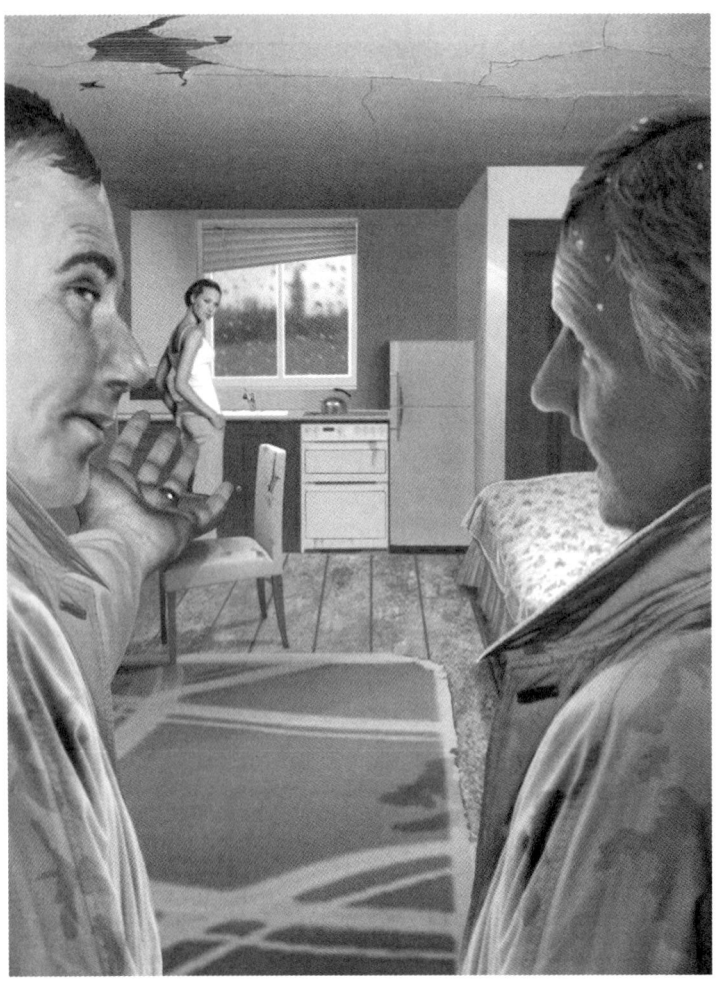

12
The Wages Fraud

Wexford was shocked into silence.

Hathall seemed to be enjoying himself. 'Why the visit?' he asked, smiling.

'You're going to Brazil,' said Wexford. 'Alone?'

'No, there'll be about three hundred other people on the plane,' said Hathall. 'I wanted Rosemary to go with me, but her school is here. Perhaps she'll come in a year or two.'

'I want to go to Europe first,' said the girl. 'I've never been.'

Hathall looked at Wexford. 'Satisfied?'

Wexford looked at him for a moment. Then he said, 'I'll have to be, Mr Hathall.'

'Then please excuse us. Rosemary and I have to get our lunch,' said Hathall.

Outside the room, the two men looked at each other. Wexford waited for Hathall to start shouting, but he didn't. The anger was in his eyes. When Wexford began to walk down the stairs, he half-saw Hathall lift his hand. Wexford moved quickly down the top three stairs, then he made himself walk slowly to the bottom.

Later that day, Howard said to Wexford, 'It wasn't his daughter all the time, Reg. Remember that I saw him outside the offices of Marcus Flower in Half Moon Street. Then he was with a blonde woman.'

'I can't follow him now. He'll be looking for me,' said Wexford.

'I can,' said Howard.

———

On the next evening, Howard Fortune was at West End Green

at six o'clock. He waited until 7.30pm, then he went along Dartmeet Avenue. There was no light in Hathall's room.

Howard was too busy to watch Hathall on Tuesday, but on Wednesday he went to Half Moon Street. He was there by five o'clock.

An hour later, he told Wexford about it.

'Hathall came out soon after 5pm,' he explained. 'I was right, Reg, it's the same man. He went down into Bond Street underground station, and I lost him. But he wasn't going home. You don't go there to go to north-west London. Bond Street is only on the Central Line.'

'Where does that go?' asked Wexford.

'East and west. He went to get a train to go west, but I lost him.'

'Where do the Central Line and the 28 bus *both* go?' asked Wexford.

'Notting Hill,' Howard said at once.

'So she lives in Notting Hill,' said Wexford.

Two days later Wexford and Howard met for dinner. 'When Hathall married Angela, they had very little money. Right?' said Howard. 'But Mark Somerset said he saw them in an expensive restaurant.'

'And he saw them shopping, with lots of parcels,' said Wexford.

'Where did Hathall get the money for that?' asked Howard. 'Is he an honest man?'

'Can a murderer ever be honest?' said Wexford. 'But ... yes, I think that he is. Mr Butler thought that he was honest.'

'But maybe Angela changed him,' said Howard. 'Maybe he did something when he was working at Kidd and Company.'

'Aveney said nothing about it.'

'You weren't asking him about money,' said Howard. 'You were asking him about women. Why don't you take another trip to Toxborough tomorrow, Reg?'

The Wages Fraud

'What happens when a new girl comes to work here, Mr Aveney?' asked Wexford. 'What do you tell the accountant?'

'I tell him her name and address,' said Aveney. 'I tell him when she's starting and the hours that she's going to work. He puts all this information into the computer.'

'Do you tell him when she leaves the job?' asked Wexford.

'Oh, yes,' replied Aveney. 'They're always leaving and going to other jobs.'

'Do some girls have their wages paid into their bank or the Post Office?'

'Yes,' said Aveney. 'And the accountant puts this information into the computer.'

'So the accountant could put a name and address into the computer. Any name and address. Wages would go into a bank account. Then the accountant, or the woman helping him, could take that money out.'

'That would be fraud,' said Aveney.

'Yes, it would,' said Wexford. 'How long do you keep the names and addresses?'

'For a year, Mr Wexford,' said Aveney. 'We keep them for a year after they leave.'

'And Hathall left them eighteen months ago,' thought Wexford. So there were no names to check.

He was driving out of the factory when he saw a police car. It was coming towards him. Wexford stopped. The police car stopped. In the back of the car was Chief Inspector Lovat of Myringham Criminal Investigation Department.

'Why are you here?' Wexford asked him.

'To do my job,' said Lovat. He was not a man to talk about his work.

'Is it about Robert Hathall?' asked Wexford.

'No,' said Lovat, smiling. 'Go on,' he told his driver.

'It would explain the money that Hathall and Angela had,' Wexford said to his nephew later. 'Money for shopping and expensive restaurants. The wages fraud was probably Angela's idea. Hathall persuades and pays another girl or woman to collect the money from the bank. The three of them do it for two years.'

'Then Hathall gets his new job, and there's no need for the wages fraud,' said Howard.

'Right,' said Wexford. 'But the other woman doesn't go away. Hathall has fallen in love with her. Angela doesn't like that. She's angry. The fraud was *her* idea. She tells Hathall that he must stop seeing the woman. Hathall pretends to agree. Then he asks his mother to come for the weekend.

'On that Friday afternoon, Angela meets with the other woman. She brings her back to Bury Cottage, perhaps to pay her for the last time. The woman strangles Angela, but leaves a print on the bath.'

'You could be right, Reg,' said Howard.

'But I can't prove any of it,' said Wexford, sadly. 'And it will soon be Christmas.'

'There's another two weeks before Christmas,' said Howard. 'I'll watch Hathall every evening that I can.'

Wexford went back to his office the next day. There was no more news about Angela's murder.

'Nancy Lake has sold her house,' said Burden, when they were having lunch at the Carousel Café. 'Some people say that she's going to live in London.'

Wexford didn't want to talk about Nancy Lake. 'I saw Lovat last week,' he told Burden. 'He didn't say much. He never does.'

'He's busy looking for a missing girl,' said Burden. 'He's almost sure that she's dead, and that her husband killed her. He's busy digging in Myringham's Old Town.'

'*Is* he?' said Wexford.

13

The Missing Woman

Wexford walked past the river in Myringham's Old Town. It was a very cold day. He saw the police cars in River Lane. They were parked in front of some empty houses. The houses had broken windows and doors. Some of them had been lived in by homeless people.

A police sergeant stood at the end of one of the gardens.

'Where's Chief Inspector Lovat, Sergeant Hutton?' asked Wexford.

'Down at the bottom of the garden, Mr Wexford,' said Hutton.

'Are they digging for the missing woman's body?'

'Yes, sir. Her name is Mrs Morag Grey. She and her husband lived here for two or three months. It was during the summer of last year. Grey has been arrested[47].'

'For murder?' said Wexford, surprised.

'For stealing from a shop,' said Hutton. 'He's going to court next week.'

Wexford walked down the garden. Lovat was sitting on a wall by the river. He was smoking a cigarette and watching his men digging.

'Why do you think that she's here?' Wexford asked him.

'She's got to be somewhere,' said Lovat.

'You think that her husband killed her, but you've got no body,' said Wexford. 'Who made you think it was him?'

'Her mother,' said Lovat.

'Let me guess,' said Wexford. 'Everyone thought that she'd gone to stay with her mother. Her mother wrote to her, but didn't get an answer. Grey was living with another woman by then. Am I right?'

The Missing Woman

'Yes,' said Lovat.

'Will you do something for me?' asked Wexford. 'You've heard about Robert Hathall. I think that he did a wages fraud when he was at Kidd and Company at Toxborough.' He explained his idea to Lovat, then he went on, 'I'm not supposed to be working on the investigation. I can't go and ask questions at the banks in Toxborough. Can you check with them for evidence of any false accounts? And do it quickly, because I've only got ten days.'

Lovat threw his cigarette on the ground. After a moment, he said, 'OK.'

Wexford walked back to his car. Suddenly, he saw Nancy Lake. She was coming out of a shop.

'Mr Wexford!' she said. 'I didn't expect to see you.'

'Can I give you a lift back to Kingsmarkham?' he said.

'Thank you, but I'm not going back just now.'

'They say that you're moving to London,' said Wexford.

'Do they?' she said. She smiled at him, and he felt his heart beat faster. 'Will you come to tea next Friday? We'll have the last of the plum jam.'

'Yes, all right,' said Wexford, after a moment.

He watched her walk away.

The Monday and Tuesday of the week before Christmas passed with nothing from Lovat. Howard had moved from West End Green to Notting Hill to watch for Hathall.

There was no news from him either.

On Wednesday morning, Wexford drove to Myringham police station.

'Chief Inspector Lovat is in court this morning,' he was told.

Wexford pushed through the crowds of Christmas shoppers to get to the court. He found a seat, then he looked around for the chief inspector. Lovat was watching the man. The man was Richard George Grey, husband of Morag.

Grey's young lawyer was talking. 'And so Mr Grey has no home,' he was saying. 'He and his wife had to leave his flat in Maynnot Hall, Toxborough. For a time he stayed in the empty house in River Lane. Then his wife left him. She said that she refused to live with a dishonest person. Where is she now? Mr Grey doesn't know, and it is a great worry to him.'

Wexford became bored with hearing more about Grey's difficulties. There was no evidence about the theft from the shop. Grey was not charged, and Lovat looked very unhappy. He got up to leave the court, and Wexford tried to follow him. But by the time he got outside, Lovat was driving away in his car. He was not going towards the police station.

Wexford decided to drive to Eileen Hathall's house in Croydon. He drove through Toxborough and along Maynnot

The Missing Woman

Way. Richard and Morag Grey had lived here, he remembered. What had the young lawyer said about Grey's wife? *She refused to live with a dishonest person.* Did that remind him of something? He couldn't remember.

Robert Hathall's mother was having lunch with Eileen Hathall. She was sitting at the table, drinking a cup of tea. She wasn't pleased to see Wexford.

'You won't find my son here,' she told him. 'He's busy getting ready to go abroad.'

'He came here last night and said goodbye,' said Eileen.

'Is he going on Monday?' asked Wexford.

'Yes,' said old Mrs Hathall. 'We shan't see him again.' She stood up and took the tea cups out to the kitchen.

'I'm glad that he's going,' Eileen said. 'Robert's mum may come to stay with me at Christmas. Rosemary is going to visit a friend in France.'

Old Mrs Hathall returned from the kitchen. 'Come on, Eileen,' she said. 'We've got dishes to wash.'

Wexford left them to do the dishes and went out of the front door. Hathall's car was outside. Rosemary was getting out of it.

'You're going to France for Christmas,' said Wexford.

She nodded but said nothing.

'You went to France before – on a school trip,' said Wexford. 'Am I right?'

'That was the day Angela was strangled,' she said coldly. 'I told my mother that I was going on the school trip. I didn't. I went out with a boy instead.'

Wexford looked at her silently for a moment. Then he said, 'You've been able to drive for eighteen months. You didn't like Angela, but you like your father ...'

'Like *him*?' she said. 'I don't like any of them. My mother is stupid, and the old woman is a cow. Do you really think that I killed Angela?' She laughed. 'There's others I'd kill first!'

―――

When Wexford got back to his office, he phoned Lovat. The chief inspector was out for the rest of the day, he was told. Soon after, Wexford went home.

Dora was making a Christmas cake. 'Do you remember asking me about a woman called Lake?' she said. 'She's getting married to a man called Somerset. His wife died two months ago. I think that he and the Lake woman have been secret lovers for years.' She looked up at him. 'Oh, don't look so unhappy, Reg!'

14
The Bank Accounts

Howard phoned at eight o'clock on Friday morning.
'I've found the bus stop, Reg,' he said.
'Tell me,' said Wexford.
'I saw Hathall leave Marcus Flower at 5.30pm,' Howard said. 'He went to Bond Street Station, so I knew that he was going to see her. I had to go back to work for an hour or two, but I got on a bus in the New King's Road by 10.30pm. I sat in the front, downstairs. And suddenly, there he was! He got on the bus in Pembridge Road and went upstairs. He got off at West End Green. I'll be at that bus stop from 5.30pm this evening, Reg.'

After breakfast, Wexford drove to Myringham police station. Lovat was there with Sergeant Hutton.

'Did you discover anything about those false bank accounts?' asked Wexford.

Lovat nodded very slowly. Then Sergeant Hutton spoke.

'We found three interesting accounts, sir,' he said. 'One was in the Trustee Savings Bank in Toxborough, one at Passingham St John, and one here in Myringham. All had money paid into them from Kidd and Company, until March or April last year. Then it stopped. The address of the woman's account in Myringham is a small hotel. The people there don't remember her, and we haven't found her. The Passingham account belonged to a woman who worked at Kidd and Company and left last March. That one was OK.'

'What about the Toxborough account?' asked Wexford.

'That's difficult, sir,' said Hutton. 'It's in the name of Mrs Mary Lewis. The address is a Toxborough address, but the people who live there have gone away. The neighbour says that they're called Kingsbury, not Lewis. But they've had people to stay with them. One of them could have been called Lewis. We'll have to wait until the Kingsburys come back.'

At four o'clock that afternoon, Wexford went to Nancy Lake's house for tea.

'Mark and I have been lovers for nineteen years,' she told him. Then she smiled at him across the table. They were sitting in an almost empty room. Most of her things were packed. She was ready to move.

'Why didn't you get married?' asked Wexford.

'We were going to marry when my husband died,' she said. 'Then Mark's wife got very ill, and he couldn't leave her.'

'You once asked me, "Is it wrong to want someone to die?"' Wexford said slowly. 'Were you thinking of his wife when you asked that?'

'Of course,' she said. 'Did you ... did you think that I was talking about *Angela*?' She laughed. 'I'll tell you something. Two years ago, I was very bored. Gwen Somerset was home from hospital and she wouldn't let Mark leave the house. So I – I flirted with Robert Hathall!'

'What did he do?' asked Wexford.

'Nothing!' she said. 'He wasn't interested in me. It was very embarrassing.'

He did not have to ask her where she had been the afternoon Angela was killed. He knew that she and Mark Somerset had been together.

December the 21st. The shortest day of the year. There were four days left until Christmas.

Howard phoned at 10pm.

'Hathall's been at Dartmeet Avenue since three o'clock,' he told Wexford. 'Alone. I'm going home now, Reg. I'll watch him again tomorrow, for the last time.'

The Bank Accounts

Wexford went to bed early. On Sunday, he stayed at home with Dora. Howard and Denise would arrive the next day for Christmas.

The phone went at 11pm.

'That'll be Howard to tell us when they're arriving,' thought Wexford.

But he was wrong. It *was* Howard, but with different news.

'I saw her,' said Howard.

'You *saw* her?' Wexford felt sick. It was too late to do anything now.

'I saw them together, but I lost them,' Howard explained. 'I started watching the house in Dartmeet Avenue after lunch. He came out of the house at 6pm. He walked down to West End Green, and I followed him in the car. I parked in Mill Lane. We both waited for about five minutes. The 28 bus didn't come, and he got a taxi instead.'

'Did you follow it?' asked Wexford.

'Yes,' said Howard. 'Hathall got out in Pembridge Road, outside a pub. It's called the Rosy Cross. He went in, and I followed him. He bought two drinks, then he found two seats in a corner. She arrived ten minutes later. It was the same woman who was with him outside Marcus Flower. A pretty woman, about thirty years old, with short blonde hair. I didn't see her hand. But I think that Hathall recognized me. Well, I have been watching him for some time now.

'They finished their drinks quickly,' Howard went on. 'Then they pushed their way out through the crowd. She must live quite near there. I saw them walking away when I came out. A taxi came and they got into it. It went up Pembridge Road, and I lost them. Sorry, Reg.'

'It's all right. Thanks, Howard.'

Then Wexford said goodnight to his nephew.

15

The Day Before Christmas Eve

It was *the* day. The day before Christmas Eve.

Wexford woke early. He thought of Hathall waking early, too.

'He saw Howard last night,' thought Wexford. 'He suspects that he's still being followed. So the woman won't be with him at 62 Dartmeet Avenue.'

He got out of bed. An hour later, he was in his office. Chief Inspector Lovat and Sergeant Hutton arrived when he was looking through his letters.

'Lovely day,' said Lovat.

'What's lovely about it?' said Wexford angrily.

The two men sat in chairs opposite Wexford. Then Hutton started speaking.

'We've got something interesting to tell you,' he said. 'We called at the home of Mr and Mrs Kingsbury again last night. They'd just returned. No, someone called Mrs Mary Lewis has never stayed with them. And we can't find any evidence of someone called Dorothy Carter. She was supposed to be the woman at the small hotel in Myringham.'

'So you want to arrest Hathall for fraud,' said Wexford. He looked at the clock. It was 10.30am. 'Well, he's probably on a plane by now.'

What made him ask the next question? Afterwards, he was never sure. He asked it when they were in Lovat's police car. They were going to see the chief constable.

'What are the addresses of the false accounts?' he asked.

'Ascot Hotel, Myringham and 19 Maynnot Way, Toxborough,' replied Hutton.

'Maynnot Way?' said Wexford. He began to get excited. 'Tell me. What were you doing at Kidd and Company the other day?'

Lovat looked at Hutton. Then Hutton said, 'Morag Grey worked there for a short time. She was a cleaner.'

'Then Morag Grey isn't buried in anybody's garden!' shouted Wexford.

'How do you know?' said Lovat.

'Because she's Robert Hathall's woman!' said Wexford. 'She's going to Brazil with him! Hathall must have met her when they both worked at Kidd and Company. She and Hathall's wife got the money out of those false accounts. She probably thought of the address of 'Mary Lewis' because Morag Grey once lived in Maynnot Way. She isn't dead. She's been living in London. When did she disappear?'

'In August or September of last year, sir,' said Hutton. He stopped the car outside Griswold's house, and the three men went inside.

The chief constable listened to them. Then he said, 'This is a little more than a "feeling", Reg.'

Then Griswold went to phone London Airport.

Wexford, Lovat and Hutton waited.

'Robert Hathall's flying to Rio de Janeiro at 12.45pm. There's a woman with him,' the chief constable said when he came back. 'We'll get the airport police to charge them with fraud, and keep them there. She's travelling as Mrs Hathall. Will she be travelling on his passport?'

'She might be travelling on Angela's,' said Wexford. 'He's still got it. I remember looking at it at Bury Cottage.'

'Well, he won't get out of the country now,' said Griswold. 'They'll stop him at the airport. Go and get him, Reg.'

First Wexford and Lovat went back to get Burden.

'Get in the car, Mike,' said Wexford. 'I'll explain everything on the way to the airport.'

The Day Before Christmas Eve

They left in two cars. In the first was Lovat, his driver and a policewoman called Polly Davis. In the second was Wexford, Burden and Hutton, with their driver.

'Tell me everything that you know about Morag Grey,' Wexford said to Hutton.

'She's from Ullapool in Scotland, sir,' replied Hutton. 'She met Grey seven or eight years ago. They got married and they both got jobs at Maynnot Hall. She was a cleaner, he worked in the garden.'

'How old is she? What does she look like?' asked Wexford.

'About thirty-two,' said Hutton. 'She's thin, with dark hair.'

'Dark hair? Well, women often changed the colour of their hair,' thought Wexford.

'She did other cleaning jobs, too,' said Hutton. 'One was at Kidd and Company. That was a year ago last March. But she only stayed two or three weeks. Then Grey lost his job. He stole money from his employer's wife's handbag. He was caught, and he and Morag had to leave their flat. They went to live at the empty house in Myringham Old Town. Then Morag found out how Grey had lost his job. After that, she wouldn't go on living with him. She said she didn't want to live with someone who was dishonest. Grey went to live with another woman on the other side of Myringham.'

'Is that Grey's story?' asked Wexford.

'Yes,' said Hutton. 'He says that he bought Morag a necklace with the money that he stole.'

A necklace. Wexford smiled.

'What happened after she sent Grey away?' asked Burden.

'She had several cleaning jobs, then she moved away. Nobody saw her after September. Her mother came down here from Scotland. She spoke Gaelic.'

'Does Morag speak Gaelic?' asked Wexford.

'Yes, sir,' said Hutton. 'Gaelic and English, her mother told us.'

16
The Woman in the Pub

It was nearly four o'clock when they got to the airport. There was thick fog, and no planes were flying. But Hathall wasn't there. Hundreds of people had phoned the airport earlier to ask about their flights. Had Hathall been one of them? They did not know.

Burden and Polly stayed at the airport. Wexford, Lovat and Hutton began the long drive to Hampstead. It was a slow journey in the fog.

At 6.50pm they stopped outside 62 Dartmeet Avenue. There was no light in Hathall's window.

'Mr Hathall left last night,' the landlord told them.

Wexford asked to see Hathall's room. The landlord took them up the stairs, but the room was empty. 'He left at about nine o'clock,' the landlord said.

Wexford went to the phone box across the road. He phoned Burden at the airport.

'He knows that we're looking for him,' said Burden. 'He phoned Aveney at his home at nine o'clock last night. He wanted to know if the police had asked questions about him and his wife. Aveney told him that they hadn't asked about him. He said that they had only asked about the girls' wages and bank accounts.'

'How do you know all this?' said Wexford.

'Aveney told Griswold. Aveney tried to phone you this morning, but you had gone.'

Wexford went back to the car.

'The fog is getting thinner, sir,' said Hutton. 'It's ten minutes to eight. Do we go back to the airport, or do we try to find Morag Grey's place?'

The Woman in the Pub

'I've been trying to do that for nine months, sergeant,' said Wexford.

'We could go back through Notting Hill, sir,' said Hutton.

'Oh, all right!' said Wexford, angrily. 'I don't care!'

He watched the road names: West End Lane, Kilburn High Road, Kilburn Park, Shirland Road, Western Road, Pembridge Villas, Pembridge Road ... Howard had seen Hathall get on the 28 bus at one of these bus stops.

Suddenly, he saw a sign outside a pub. The pub was called The Rosy Cross. This was the pub where Howard had seen Hathall and the blonde-haired woman together!

'Stop the car!' he said quickly.

He jumped out and hurried into the pub. It was crowded inside and it was difficult to get to the bar.

'Police,' he told the barman. 'I'm looking for a tall black-haired young man, and a younger blonde woman. They were in here last night.'

'There were five hundred people in here last night,' said the barman.

'I think that they come here often,' said Wexford.

'Listen, I'm busy,' replied the barman. 'Can you wait ten minutes?'

But Wexford had waited too long already. He started to go back to the door. It was hot in the pub and his head hurt. He pushed through the crowd. There were heads everywhere.

A blonde head.

There were too many people between him and the corner table. But he could see her. A girl with blonde hair. *He could see her.*

She had a tired but pretty face under the short blonde hair. She was alone, but there was a man's coat on the chair next to her. Around her feet were six suitcases. She had a drink in front of her, but she was looking nervously towards a door. The sign on the door said: *Telephone and Toilets.*

The Woman in the Pub

Wexford waited. When other people moved in front of her, he opened the door. There was a telephone box at the end of the room. Hathall was inside it.

'He's phoning the airport,' thought Wexford. 'He's asking about his flight, now that the fog is thinner.'

Wexford went quickly into the men's toilet, and waited. After a minute, he heard Hathall go past the door and back into the bar. He waited another minute, then he went back into the bar. The suitcases had gone.

Wexford moved through the crowd and pushed the street door open. Hathall and the woman were standing on the pavement with their suitcases. They were waiting for a taxi. Wexford pointed at them – and three of the police car's doors opened at the same time. The three policemen moved quickly.

Hathall saw them and the colour went out of his face. Wexford went across.

The woman saw him. 'It's too late, Robert,' she said. And when Wexford heard her voice, *he knew*. But he let Lovat go to her.

'Morag Grey ... ' Lovat began.

She put a shaking hand up to her mouth – and Wexford saw the small L-shaped scar on her forefinger.

The woman saw him. 'It's too late, Robert,' she said.

17
The Last Surprise

It was Christmas Eve, and most of Wexford's family had arrived. They were in various rooms of the house. Wexford and Howard were alone in the dining room. They were sitting comfortably by the fire.

'She was living in Pembridge Road,' Wexford was saying. 'In a flat. He had that sad little room, but he paid her rent as well. What has Mike Burden told you, Howard?'

'He's told me that the woman's name is Morag Grey,' said Howard. 'And that the three of them worked the fraud. Was that right?'

'There's more to tell you,' said Wexford. 'Yes, there was a wages fraud. Hathall arranged two false accounts soon after he went to work at Kidd and Company. He probably arranged more. But Morag Grey wasn't part of the fraud. She was an honest woman. She only worked at Kidd and Company for two weeks. That was three months before Hathall left.'

'But Hathall was in love with her. You said that – '

'Hathall was in love with his wife,' said Wexford. 'He's *still* in love with her.'

'I don't understand,' said Howard. 'You'll be saying in a minute that Morag Grey didn't kill Angela Hathall.'

'That's right,' said Wexford. 'She didn't. *Angela Hathall killed Morag Grey.*'

'What!' said Howard.

'I guessed yesterday,' said Wexford, 'First, Hutton told me that Morag Grey was only at Kidd and Company for a very short time. He said that she was a very honest woman. She wouldn't even stay with Grey after he stole money from their employer.

'Then,' Wexford went on, 'outside the pub, I heard the blonde woman speak. She sounded *Australian*.'

Howard looked amazed. 'What about the identification of the body?'

'Remember, Angela Hathall had no friends,' said Wexford. 'Mrs Lake knew her, and so did Mark Somerset. But we weren't likely to ask them to identify the body. Hathall knew that we would ask *him* to identify it.'

'But his mother saw the body,' said Howard.

'Old Mrs Hathall met Angela once, at Earl's Court. On that day, Angela was wearing jeans and a red shirt. And the body at Bury Cottage was *face-down* – dressed in *jeans and a red shirt*.'

'Very clever!' said Howard.

'Angela started cleaning the house weeks before her mother-in-law's visit,' Wexford went on. 'She had to clean off *her own fingerprints*. She missed the handprint on the bath. That and the L-shaped scar were hers. The fingerprints that we *thought* were hers were Morag's.'

'How did Angela first meet Morag?' asked Howard.

'Morag Grey spoke Gaelic. Hathall must have discovered this. So Angela wrote to her. She pretended to need help with her study of Celtic languages. Morag needed the money that Angela promised to pay her.'

'But didn't she know that Angela was Hathall's wife?'

'No, she didn't. Angela gave her a false name. And Morag didn't know that Hathall lived at Bury Cottage. On the 19th of September, Angela drove to Myringham Old Town. She collected Morag and drove her back to Bury Cottage. She took her upstairs to wash or use the toilet. Then she strangled her with Morag's own necklace. Next, she dressed Morag in the red shirt and jeans, and put her face-down on the bed. Then she left the house. She drove to London and stayed a night or two in a hotel. After that, she rented a room to use until Hathall could meet with her.'

The Last Surprise

'But *why*, Reg?' said Howard. 'Why did they kill her?'

'Morag found out about the wages fraud,' Wexford replied.

'How?'

'I'm not sure,' said Wexford. 'Morag was a cleaner at Kidd and Company. Maybe Hathall stayed late at his office one night. Maybe he was talking to Angela on the phone about the wages fraud, and Morag heard him. Maybe Hathall said the name Mary Lewis, and that address, 19 Maynnot Way. Morag and her husband stayed just down the road from there. She probably knew the people at number nineteen. She probably knew that nobody called Mary Lewis was living there.'

'Did she ask Hathall for money?' said Howard. 'To stay silent?'

'No, I don't think so,' said Wexford. 'She was honest. But she probably asked him questions. She probably told him she knew that there was no Mary Lewis at number nineteen. Then he got nervous and worried. He thought she would ask more and more questions until she understood everything.'

'They killed her for *that*?' said Howard.

Wexford nodded. 'It seems crazy. But Hathall was afraid that he would lose his job, and the new job at Marcus Flower. He was afraid that he'd never get a job as an accountant again. That he would go to prison and not see Angela again. For Robert and Angela, that was more than enough reason for murder.'

Points for Understanding

1

1 Where are Robert and Mrs Hathall going? Why?
2 Why doesn't Mrs Hathall like Angela?
3 What does Wexford think of Robert Hathall? Why?

2

1 How does Hathall react to Wexford's questions?
2 Why is Hathall looking at the newspaper?
3 Describe the different fingerprints found in the house.

3

1 How do we know that Wexford is interested in Nancy Lake? Give examples from their meeting at the police station.
2 Wexford thinks that Hathall's behaviour was strange on the day his wife's body was found. In what way?

4

1 List four things that Eileen did when Hathall asked for a divorce.
2 Who owns Bury Cottage? How did Robert and Angela Hathall come to live there?
3 Why did Hathall decide to live with his mother during the week?

5

1 Both Mark Somerset and Robert Hathall explain about the rent that the Hathalls paid for Bury Cottage. How are their stories different?
2 How did Mark Somerset feel about his cousin?
3 'No. It was Angela's book,' said Hathall. 'She's had it for years.' Why was this a strange thing for Hathall to say?

6

1. At the beginning of the chapter, where are these people planning to go for lunch?
   (a) Nancy Lake (b) Wexford.
2. Give three pieces of information on where the L-shaped scar is from.

7

1. Where do the Wexfords stay during their visit to London?
2. What do these people say about Robert Hathall?
   (a) Jason Marcus and Stephen Flower (b) Linda Kipling.
3. What is the 'very small fraud' that Marie Marcovitch is talking about? What does it have to do with Angela Hathall?

8

1. What does William Butler say about these people?
   (a) Jonathan Craig (b) Robert Hathall (c) Angela Hathall (d) Eileen Hathall.
2. What two pieces of news does Burden have for Wexford?
3. Why does Rosemary Hathall hate her father?
4. Why does Griswold order Wexford to stay away from Hathall?

9

1. How do these different policemen think Angela Hathall was killed?
   (a) Burden (b) Wexford (c) Griswold.
2. Why does Wexford think Hathall has moved to north-west London?
3. In the beginning, how often does Ginge Matthews work on the case? How does Wexford pay him?
4. What does Wexford read on the back page of the newspaper?

10

1 Describe the woman that Howard Fortune saw with Hathall.
2 In this chapter, the phrase in the title of the book, 'Shake Hands For Ever', is mentioned for the first time. Why?
3 Which two aspects of his investigation into Hathall must Wexford keep from Griswold? Why?

11

1 Where does Wexford go for his two-week holiday? Why?
2 Why does Ginge stop helping Wexford?
3 Who is the girl in Hathall's flat?

12

1 'Wexford moved quickly down the top three stairs'. Why?
2 What, if anything, does Howard find out about Hathall on these days?
   (a) Monday   (b) Tuesday   (c) Wednesday.
3 When a new girl starts work at Kidd and Company, what five pieces of information does the accountant put into the computer?
4 Why does Wexford need to prove that Hathall is guilty before Christmas?

13

1 Why has Richard Grey been arrested?
2 What does Wexford ask Lovat to do? How long does he give him to do it? Why can't he do it himself?
3 Where was Rosemary Hathall on the day Angela was murdered?

14

1 What information do Lovat and Hutton find about these three bank accounts?
   (a) Toxborough   (b) Passingham St John   (c) Myringham.
2 How long have Mark Somerset and Nancy Lake been lovers? Why haven't they got married until now?
3 What did Hathall and the woman do when they saw Howard watching them?

15

1 Why does Wexford get excited when Hutton mentions Maynnot Way?
2 What does Griswold do when he hears Wexford's new information?
3 What did Morag Grey do as soon as she found out her husband was a thief?

16

1 Why hasn't Hathall's plane left yet?
2 Who do these people phone, or try to phone, between 9pm on the 22nd December and the same time on the 23rd? Why?
   (a) Hathall (2 calls)   (b) Aveney (2 calls)   (c) Wexford (1 call).
3 What is The Rosy Cross? Why is it important to the story?

17

1 Who is the murdered woman?
2 What do these things have to do with the murder?
   (a) Wages   (b) Jeans and a red shirt   (c) The L-shaped scar
   (d) A necklace   (e) Gaelic.

Glossary

1. ***crime*** (page 4)
   a *crime* is an illegal activity or action. Someone who has committed a crime is a *criminal*.
2. ***Detective Inspector*** (page 4)
   a senior police officer whose job is to try to discover information about a crime.
3. ***fiction*** (page 4)
   books and stories about events and people that are not real.
4. ***murder*** (page 4)
   the crime of deliberately killing someone.
5. ***evidence*** (page 5)
   when a crime has been *committed*, there is an *investigation*. This is the process of trying to find out all the facts about something in order to discover who or what caused it or how it happened. A policeman looks for *clues* – objects or facts that help to solve a crime or mystery. Clues help to prove whether someone has committed a crime and are called *evidence*.
6. ***stubborn*** (page 6)
   not willing to change your ideas or decisions.
7. ***fault*** (page 9)
   something that makes someone or something less good.
8. ***in-laws*** (page 9)
   the parents or other relatives of your husband or wife. The wife of your son is your *daughter-in-law*, and the mother of your husband is your *mother-in-law*.
9. ***greedy*** (page 9)
   wanting more money, possessions, or power than you need.
10. ***widow*** (page 10)
    a woman whose husband has died.
11. ***cottage*** (page 10)
    a small old house in a village or in the countryside.
12. ***fingerprint*** (page 12)
    a mark on something that you have touched that shows the pattern of lines on your fingers. A *handprint* is a mark that shows all of your hand.
13. ***sympathy*** (page 12)
    a feeling of kindness and understanding that you have for someone who is experiencing problems.

14 **accountant** (page 13)
someone whose job is to prepare or check financial records, or *accounts*.
15 **strangled** – *to strangle someone* (page 14)
to kill a person or an animal by squeezing their throat.
16 **ashamed** (page 16)
feeling guilty or embarrassed about something that you have done.
17 **case** (page 18)
a crime that the police are investigating. When someone dies, there is an *inquest*. This is an official attempt by a court to find the cause of someone's death. The official decision made by the court is called the *verdict*.
18 **glove** (page 18)
a piece of clothing that covers your fingers and hand.
19 **scar** (page 18)
a permanent mark on your skin where you have been injured.
20 **plum** (page 20)
a small round fruit with purple, red, or yellow skin and a large hard stone inside.
21 **persuaded** – *to persuade someone to do something* (page 23)
to make someone agree to do something by giving them reasons why they should.
22 **jewellery** (page 24)
objects that you wear as decoration. A *bracelet* is a piece of jewellery that you wear around your wrist. You wear *rings* on your fingers and a *necklace* round your neck.
23 **thief** (page 24)
someone who steals something. *Theft* is the crime of stealing something.
24 **refused** – *to refuse* (page 25)
to say that you will not do or accept something, or will not let someone do something.
25 **sacked** – *to sack someone* (page 25)
to force someone to leave their job.
26 **stress** (page 25)
a worried or nervous feeling that makes you unable to relax, or a situation that makes you feel like this.
27 **mean** (page 30)
not willing to spend money.

28 **parcel** (page 30)
the things you have bought in a shop, wrapped in paper or held in bags so that they can be carried. Robert and Angela say that they do not have a lot of money, but the parcels show that this is not true.

29 **Gaelic** (page 32)
a Celtic language that people speak in parts of Scotland and Ireland. The Celts were an ancient group of people who lived in parts of Western Europe.

30 **flirting** – *to flirt with someone* (page 34)
to behave towards someone in a way that shows that you are sexually attracted to them.

31 **satisfied** (page 35)
pleased with what has happened, or with what you have achieved.

32 **threaten** (page 37)
to tell someone that you will cause them harm or problems, especially in order to make them do something.

33 **fraud** (page 37)
the crime of obtaining money from someone by tricking them.

34 **dummy** (page 38)
a model of a person's body, often used to show clothes in shops.

35 **sick** (page 39)
if you are sick, you have an illness.

36 **complained** – *to complain* (page 39)
to say that you are not satisfied with something.

37 **retired** (page 41)
no longer working at a job, especially when you are old.

38 **break the law** – *to break the law* (page 42)
to do something that is not allowed by the law.

39 **honest** (page 42)
a person who is honest does not tell lies or cheat people, and obeys the law. The opposite of honest is *dishonest*.

40 **guilty** (page 47)
someone who is guilty has committed a crime or has done something wrong. The opposite of guilty is *innocent*.

41 **identify** – *to identify* (page 49)
to recognize someone and be able to say who they are.

42 **wages** (page 51)
a regular amount of money that you earn for working.

43 ***digging*** – *to dig* (page 55)
to make a hole in the earth using your hands, a machine, or a tool.
44 ***cesspit*** (page 55)
a large hole under the ground for collecting liquid and solid waste that comes from a building.
45 ***drainage*** (page 55)
a system of pipes and passages that take away water or waste liquid from an area.
46 ***prove*** – *to prove* (page 56)
to provide evidence that shows that something is true.
47 ***arrested*** – *to arrest someone* (page 65)
if the police arrest someone, they take that person to a police station because they think that he or she has committed a crime. The person who has been arrested is taken to a *court* – a place where trials take place and legal cases are decided, and if the court decides that they have done something wrong, they are *charged* – accused officially of committing a crime.

Dictionary extracts adapted from the Macmillan English Dictionary © Macmillan Publishers Limited 2002.

Exercises

The author: true or false?

Read the statements about Ruth Rendell. Write T (True) or F (False).

1 She writes stories about crime.	T
2 Her books are published in 35 languages.	
3 All of her books have been televised.	
4 She writes fiction.	
5 Her first novel was published in 1964.	
6 Her great-grandmother was also a writer.	
7 She also writes novels using a different name.	
8 She has never won an award for her writing.	
9 Not all of her books include a murder.	
10 She writes two books every year.	

Background

Finish the sentences 1–8 with the correct information. The first one is an example.

1	Wexford lives in	a	called Dora.
2	Kingsmarkham is a very	b	from a poem by Drayton.
3	Wexford wants to know	c	Kingsmarkham.
4	Wexford isn't interested in	d	man to live with.
5	Wexford doesn't like	e	beautiful country town.
6	Wexford has a wife	f	big cities.
7	Wexford is a difficult	g	forensic evidence.
8	The title of the book comes	h	why people commit crimes.

People in the story

Complete the sentences with a name from the box.

> Mark Somerset   ~~Burden~~   Nancy Lake   Angela
> Eileen   Howard Fortune   Ginge Matthews   Charles Griswold
> Morag Grey   Lovat   Rosemary

1 Wexford worked with Inspector .... *Burden* ....
2 Wexford's boss was called ....
3 Robert Hathall's wife was called ....
4 Robert Hathall's daughter was called ....
5 Rosemary's mother was called ....
6 Angela's cousin was called ....
7 Wexford had a nephew called ....
8 Wexford employed a man called ....
9 Mark Somerset was in love with ....
10 Wexford got help from Chief Inspector ....
11 Robert and Angela killed ....

Vocabulary: adjectives

a Match the adjectives in the box to their OPPOSITES below. The first one is an example.

> cruel   calm   shy   nervous   ashamed   ~~guilty~~   secretive
> satisfied   honest   stubborn

1 innocent ..... *guilty* .....   6 open   ....
2 dishonest ....   7 kind   ....
3 flexible ....   8 dissatisfied ....
4 proud   ....   9 relaxed   ....
5 outgoing ....   10 stressed   ....

b Match the descriptions below to an adjective from part a. The first one is done for you.

1 Wexford wasn't happy with Hathall's explanation. ...*dissatisfied*...

2 Angela committed the crime. ....

3 Eileen enjoyed making Angela unhappy. ....

4 Morag always told the truth. ....

5 Wexford could not be persuaded to forget Hathall. ....

6 Nancy didn't want to tell Wexford everything. ....

7 Hathall lied to Wexford about his wife. ....

8 Angela didn't like meeting people. ....

9 Hathall got worried when Morag Grey started asking questions. ....

10 Richard Grey felt very bad about the theft. ....

Vocabulary: crime and the law

Write the words in the box in the gaps. Change the verb form when necessary. The first one is done for you.

> fingerprints   footprints   evidence   strangle   case
> inquest   verdict   investigation   fraud   identify
> prove   arrest   court   lawyer   ~~inspector~~
> break the law   follow

Wexford is an (1) ......*inspector*...... . When a crime is committed, or someone (2) ...., Wexford begins an (3) .... Each crime that the police investigate is called a (4)...................... . This means that they try to find clues in order to find the guilty person. Clues could include (5) .... or (6) .... and the clues are called (7) .... Sometimes, the police (8) .... people to find out where they are going, or

93

sometimes a person can (9) .... the possible criminal because they saw him or her at the time and place of the crime.

If somebody dies for no clear reason, it is necessary to find out how they died by having an (10) .... In the story, Angela (11) .... Morag by pulling on a necklace around her neck. She did this because Morag knew that she was stealing money from the company and this is called (12) .... When the police think they have found the person, they (13) .... him or her and then they go to a place called a (14) ...., where he or she is called the accused. The accused needs a person called a (15) ...., who tries to (16) .... that he or she is innocent. At the end, there are two choices: the person is guilty or innocent – this is called a (17) ....

Words from the story

Match the words on the left to the definitions on the right. The first one is done for you.

1	sympathy *i*	a	to stop working when you are 60–65
2	faults	b	a person who lives in a flat or house near you
3	a stranger	c	to promise you will do something bad
4	a lane	d	to say you do not want to do something
5	gloves	e	to make a hole in the ground
6	a neighbour	f	a model of a person, often used to show clothes in shops
7	to persuade	g	a large hole underground for old, dirty water from the house, eg from the bathroom or toilet
8	a scar	h	to want more of something that you need, eg food or money

9	to wipe	i	~~a feeling of understanding for a person's problems~~
10	to sack	j	a small road, often in the countryside
11	to refuse	k	a person you don't know
12	to retire	l	to say or do things to show you are sexually interested in another person
13	to flirt	m	things you wear on your hands and fingers to cover them
14	to threaten	n	things which are wrapped in paper and posted or bought from a shop
15	to complain	o	an old language which is spoken in parts of Scotland and Ireland
16	to dig	p	to be ill
17	Gaelic	q	pipes which carry old, dirty water away from the house
18	a parcel	r	to try to use words and reasons to make someone do something
19	a cesspit	s	a mark on your skin after you cut it, for example, which will always be there
20	to be sick	t	to move your hand in the air when saying hello or goodbye
21	drainage	u	to say you are not happy with something
22	to wave	v	to clean something dirty with a cloth, eg in the house
23	a dummy	w	to tell someone they must leave their job because they did something wrong
24	to be greedy	x	things which make a person or thing worse

Pronunciation: stress

Put the words into the correct stress pattern boxes. Four words are done for you.

> ~~refuse~~ ~~sympathy~~ ~~verdict~~ ~~detective~~ retire secretive
> guilty arrest greedy forensic inquest inspector
> threaten evidence ashamed arrested stubborn persuade
> satisfied dishonest innocent complain

o O	O o
refuse	verdict

O o o	o O o
sympathy	detective

Grammar: the passive

a What are the past simple forms and past participles of these irregular verbs?

Infinitive	Past simple	Past participle
1 take		
2 find		
3 leave		
4 see		
5 steal		

b Rewrite the sentences in the passive (*was/were (not)* + past participle).

> **Example 1:** *The police took fingerprints.*
> *Fingerprints were taken.*
>
> **Example 2:** *Someone told the police about the murder.*
> *The police were told about the murder.*

1 Someone strangled Angela.

2 Someone found her in the bedroom.

3 Someone sacked Robert from work.

4 They left fingerprints in the house.

5 Someone left hairs in the bathroom.

6 Someone cleaned the house very well.

7 Someone stole the car from the garage.

8 They suspected the Hathalls of breaking the law.

9 Someone planned the murder.

10 They asked Robert to identify the body.

11 They didn't find the car in Kingsmarkham.

12 Someone saw Robert with a girl.

13 They found the necklace in a cesspit.

14 They didn't arrest Grey.

15 They stopped the planes because of the weather.

16 They arrested Angela and Robert.

Multiple choice

Tick the best answer. The first one is done for you.

1 How did Mrs Hathall feel about her son's marriage to Angela?
   a She was against it.   ✓
   b She thought it was a good idea.
   c She didn't feel strongly about it.

2 Where did Wexford expect Robert Hathall to go when he got home?
   a To the garage.
   b To the living room.
   c To the bedroom.

3 Who was Nancy Lake in love with?
   a Her husband.
   b Mark Somerset.
   c Wexford.

4 Where was Robert Hathall at the time of the murder?
   a In Kingsmarkham.
   b At work.
   c On a train.

5 What was Robert Hathall most worried about?
   a Fingerprints.
   b Footprints.
   c The book about languages.

6 Why did Charles Griswold tell Wexford not to continue with the case?
   a He had a different idea about the murder.
   b He didn't like Wexford.
   c He thought Wexford didn't have enough evidence.

7 Why did Ginge Matthews refuse to follow Robert Hathall?
   a Hathall had hit him.
   b He didn't need the job anymore.
   c He argued with Wexford.

8 Who saw Robert and Angela Hathall together in London?
   a Ginge Matthews.
   b Howard Fortune.
   c Lovat.

9 Who was Wexford surprised to see in Robert Hathall's London flat?
   a Eileen.
   b Angela.
   c Rosemary.

10 How did Robert Hathall know Morag Grey?
   a She cleaned for him.
   b She helped him to steal money from the company.
   c She worked at the same company as him.

Published by Macmillan Heinemann ELT
Between Towns Road, Oxford OX4 3PP
A division of Macmillan Publishers Limited
Companies and representatives throughout the world
Heinemann is the registered trademark of Pearson Education, used under licence.

ISBN 978–0–2307–2263–7
ISBN 978–0–2307–3213–1 (with CD pack)

This version of *Shake Hands For Ever* by Ruth Rendell was retold by
John Escott for Macmillan Readers

© Kingsmarkham Enterprises Limited, 2002
First published in the UK by Hutchinson, one of the publishers in the
Random House Group

First published 2009
Text © Macmillan Publishers Limited 2009
Design and illustration © Macmillan Publishers Limited 2009

All rights reserved; no part of this publication may be
reproduced, stored in a retrieval system, transmitted in any
form, or by any means, electronic, mechanical, photocopying,
recording, or otherwise, without the prior written permission of
the publishers.

Illustrated by Peter Harper and Simon Williams
Cover photograph by Corbis/William Whitehurst

Printed and bound in Thailand

2011 2010 2009
6 5 4 3 2

with CD pack
2011 2010 2009
5 4 3 2 1